PUSHKIN'S

I. P. BELKIN

Andrej Kodjak

New York University

PUSHKIN'S

I. P. BELKIN

Andrej Kodjak

New York University

1979

Slavica Publishers, Inc.

Columbus, Ohio

For a complete catalog of other books from Slavica, with prices and ordering information, write to:

SLAVICA PUBLISHERS, INC.
P.O. Box 14388
Columbus, Ohio 43214

ISBN: 0-89357-057-5.

Editor of Slavica Publishers: Charles E. Gribble, The Ohio State University, Columbus.

Type set by Charles Press, Inc., 161 Grand Street, New York, N.Y. 10013.

Printed in the United States of America by LithoCrafters, Inc., Chelsea, Michigan 48118.

CONTENTS

INTRODUCTION

Puškin's three-month confinement to his estate in 1830, his "Boldino autumn," has come to be viewed as perhaps the most important period in his literary life. His achievement during these months in virtually all genres—lyrical and narrative poetry, prose, and drama—remained unmatched. This artistic outburst occurred in one of the most disturbed periods of Puškin's later years when he was facing the prospect of marriage to Natalja Gončarova, who six years later would cause the duel resulting in his death. Puškin's relationship with the Gončarov family was difficult, to say the least, and his financial situation was far from secure. In addition to these anxieties and difficulties, he felt the heavy hand of Emperor Nicholas I, his personal censor, who assumed the throne after having suppressed the Decembrist revolt of 1825 as a result of which many of Puškin's close friends were prosecuted. With all of these thoughts, worries and uncertainties Puškin was trapped in Boldino because of a cholera epidemic and the subsequent quarantine which had halted travel throughout the region. Only after the roads were reopened was Puškin able to leave Boldino. He arrived in Moscow on December 5, 1830, with an impressive stack of manuscripts, including a collection of five short stories, *The Tales of Belkin*, with a foreword, containing Belkin's biography. It is exactly this foreword, "From the Editor," which is the point of investigation in this study. The numerous contradictions, omissions and allusions in the foreword lead to the conclusion that this short (only 1015 words) text contains an elaborate code. Its decoding is the aim of the present study.

*　　*　　*

The Tales of Belkin, published anonymously in 1831, marked Puškin's debut in prose. It was coldly received by the critics,[1] including Belinsky, and for a long time was ignored by literary scholars. The critics thought the five stories allegedly written by Ivan Petrovič Belkin shallow and naive, the personality of Belkin uninteresting, and his role as a fictitious author superfluous. Only the suggestion of A. Grigor'ev (1859)[2] that Belkin was the central figure in this cycle of short stories through whom Puškin introduced the allegedly typical, humble and unpretentious Russian man into literature triggered the interest of scholars and generated a reexamination of the entire cycle and the personality of

Belkin in particular. Although today Grigoriev's interpretation of Belkin's personality and role in the short story cycle is seen as nothing more than a historical landmark, it served a significant purpose in focusing the critics' attention on the seemingly superfluous fictitious author. V. V. Vinogradov assesses Grigor'ev's role in the literary criticism of Belkin as follows:

> A. Grigoriev's idea influenced the shape and the direction of subsequent critical speculations (especially the views of N. Straxov and Dostoevsky) concerning the nature of I. P. Belkin.
>
> Since then historians of Russian literature considered their major task in analyzing *The Tales of Belkin* solving the problem of the Puškin-Belkin relationship. Some scholars, for example, N. Kotljarevskij, L. Polivanov, N. Lerner, D. N. Ovsjaniko-Kulikovskij and others, have supported the theory of Belkin's authorship, his essential separation and isolation from Puškin. On the contrary, other critics have denied any trace of Belkin in the style of *The Tales of Belkin* and have identified the stories with Puškin exclusively.[3]

The latter point of view Vinogradov ascribes to the works of N. I. Černjaev, A. S. Iskoz and V. V. Gippius. Vinogradov sees a third group of scholars (V. F. Bocjalovskij, V. V. Gippius and N. Ljubovič) treating *The Tales of Belkin* as basically a literary parody. Vinogradov himself approaches *The Tales of Belkin* as a complex interaction of several narrative styles: those of the narrators from whom Belkin acquired his stories, his own style and finally Puškin's. Although Vinogradov's study of *The Tales* is of great value, it, nevertheless, leads to no definite conclusions.

N. V. Izmajlov in *Puškin—itogi i problemy izučenija* surveys the works on *The Tales of Belkin* as part of Puškin's entire prose effort and summarizes the attempts to solve the problem of Belkin:

> There is no homogeneous understanding of the author's [Belkin's] image in *The Tales*, his significance, as well as the role of the narrators, to whom the editor refers. . . . Are the tales written in a single style from a single literary and ideological viewpoint, i.e. from the point of view of Puškin himself, or does each of them reflect to some degree the personality of its 'narrator,' and together do they reflect the personality of Belkin? This problem demands attentive and objective examination.[4]

Belkin's personality, as A. G. Gukasova notes, has been interpreted in various ways.

> *Belkin* was perceived as: a humble, shy man of common sense and
> reason (A. Grigor'ev, L. Polivanov); a parody on Puškin or Puškin
> himself (N. Černjaev); a kind, sentimental man, a writer and phi-
> lanthropist who relaxed his control over his serfs (N. Kotljarevskij);
> a second version of Mitrofan Skotinin [a simpleton in Fonvizin's
> comedy, *The Minor*] (Uzin); an eccentric, a writer, a simple-
> minded philistine (Gippius).[5]

Still no light is shed on Belkin's function in the cycle.

Russian criticism, as V. S. Uzin bluntly states, reached a dead end
concerning the problem of Belkin:

> And so, one or the other: either the foreword is simply a mechan-
> ical addition to the tales, and in this case there is no need to search
> for an intrinsic connection between Belkin's personality and the tales
> themselves, or the foreword is an indispensable part of the entire
> cycle—in which case every element in the entire text, referred
> to as *The Tales of Ivan Petrovič Belkin*, influences neighboring
> elements and, furthermore, influences the entire system of *The
> Tales*; . . .[6]

Uzin's point is especially important for this study because he is one of
the first to suggest that Belkin's personality be analyzed with reference
to the whole text taken as an organic unit. This approach suggests that
the foreword, "From the Editor," should be read, not merely as a separate informative text, but as part of the entire artistic body of the cycle.

Uzin's insistence that the foreword be perceived as an integral part
of the whole text was not entirely new. This had already been hinted
at for extra-literary reasons, as will be shown later, by a reviewer in *The
Northern Bee* in 1831. At that time the foreword was referred to as a
"sixth tale," since the entire cycle was said to contain, instead of five, six
stories or anecdotes. Gukasova, addressing herself to the text of the foreword in her study of *The Tales of Belkin*,[7] refers to the allusions in *The
Northern Bee* as does S. G. Bočarov later.[8] The term itself is used by
Jan M. Meijer in his article, "The Sixth Tale of Belkin."[9]

Meijer and Bočarov in their brief outlines of critical studies of *The
Tales of Belkin* limit themselves to those focusing on the "sixth tale" and
on Belkin himself. Meijer's study is most pertinent to the present work,
for in the second section of his article he closely examines the structure
of the foreword. Several of Meijer's observations have direct bearing on
this study. He establishes a definite plot in the foreword, including the
editor's text preceding the neighbor's letter,[10] points out the missing information concerning the way Belkin's manuscript reached the editor,[11]

establishes Puškin's intentional omission of this information by comparing his final version with his first draft, and finally raises the question whether the alleged reason for publishing Belkin's biography as an attempt to satisfy the curiosity of the reader is not merely a pretext for Puškin to introduce the sixth tale, the foreword, which consequently must serve some function other than that claimed by the editor, A.P.[12] Although Meijer did not come to the conclusion that the foreword is a coded text, his approach brought him to the very edge of this hypothesis.

Bočarov in his recent work also touches upon some of the central points developed in this study. He singles out one of Vinogradov's important insights, namely that Belkin stands as an "algebraic sign in front of his tales."[13] That makes the five stories virtually incomprehensible without a thorough understanding of the figure of Belkin. The fictional author of the five tales, according to Bočarov, is a very special type of literary mystification. "Belkin is indeed problematic. He turns out to be inaccessible and difficult to analyze. He presents an artistic reality that escapes the available critical detectors."[14] This most important observation for the present study is further developed by Bočarov when he regards the failure of literary critics to solve the problem of Belkin: ". . . the history of this problem indicates that literary scholarship lacks appropriate approaches to a phenomenon of this type."[15] Belkin, as a literary mystery that cannot be solved by traditional critical methods, implies that the entire text of the foreword must be treated as an elaborate code. Bočarov almost arrives at the notion of a coded text when trying to establish the degree of reliability of the information about Belkin:

> . . . the information about Ivan Petrovič Belkin which is conveyed (biography, disposition, appearance) creates some human definitude, however, to a very limited degree. To solve the artistic problem of Belkin means exactly to establish the degree of his definitude, or the degree of his indefiniteness. However, the compositional devices of the foreword are purposely aimed at hindering such a solution, so that any definitude would remain dubious.

Bočarov further refers to Vinogradov: ". . . all the attention of the biographer is aimed away from literature."[16] Belkin's biographer, his neighbor, instead of giving a biography of a writer, describes Belkin as an unsuccessful landowner. This discrepancy between the biographer's alleged intentions and his final product creates those characteristics of Belkin which, as Bočarov states, escape traditional literary analysis and which would seem to suggest the presence of a code. Finally, in referring to Belkin's allegedly feeble imagination, Bočarov raises the question of the interrelation of fact and fiction in the stories.[17] This question assumes particular importance, as will be shown, in the foreword which contains a veiled reference to actual facts beneath a layer of fiction.

For the purposes of the present study, the critical works on *The Tales of Belkin* might be divided, according to their treatment of the foreword, into three categories. The first contains the majority of critical studies on *The Tales of Belkin*. These deal with individual stories taken out of the context of the entire cycle and, therefore, bypass the foreword and the question of Belkin's authorship. This category of works has little relevance for the present study which is primarily concerned with the foreword. To the second category belong critical works on *The Tales of Belkin*, which while analyzing the entire cycle do not consistently regard the foreword as an integral part of it, i.e. do not view the text, "From the Editor," as a sixth story written by a second fictional author, the editor, A.P. These works, likewise, have little relevance for the present study. The third category contains only a few studies. Here the entire text of *The Tales of Belkin*, including the foreword, is regarded as an integrated artistic unit. These works share with the present study certain basic assumptions, the complexity and ambiguity of the foreword being perhaps the most important. In chronological order these works are by Uzin, Vinogradov, Meijer and Bočarov. Of these, the works of the last two scholars, published in 1968 and 1974 respectively, stand in direct relation to the present study, since they uncompromisingly incorporate the foreword as part of the artistic unity of *The Tales of Belkin*. In 1970 my article entitled "Puškin's Code," *Šifr Puškina*,[18] dealing with the foreword, was published, but in all probability it remained unknown to Bočarov. Thus the attempts to treat *The Tales of Belkin* as a cycle comprised of six artistic units, or six short stories, are few and relatively recent.

The different interpretations of Belkin's personality, no matter how far removed from one another, still have a common denominator. The foreword and the fictional author are generally regarded as Puškin's literary game, invented for one or another reason according to established literary patterns (in this case after Sir Walter Scott, as D. P. Jakubovič pointed out in 1926).[19] The findings of the present study indicate, however, that the foreword was constructed by Puškin in an entirely new fashion, with the application of an elaborate cipher which must be decoded in order to understand Belkin and his function in the cycle of tales accurately. The foreword cannot be regarded as a literary game but rather as a rare artistic phenomenon combining characteristics of fiction and a coded historical account under exceptionally harsh censorship. The analysis of such a text demands the reexamination of each detail

—the more insignificant the detail, the more likelihood of its importance in the code—and establishing its relation to the remaining details in the text, as well as to the extratextual facts. All the findings must be presented in their entirety in the absence of supportive material by other critics. Such a presentation threatens to become lengthy but cannot be shortened in view of the conflict between the findings of the present study and the traditional literary treatment of the problem of Belkin.

In order to facilitate the reader's following the multitude of details essential to the present study, the decoding of the foreword, "From the Editor," is presented in the first chapter and the history of the writing and the publishing of the tales by Puškin in the last chapter.

Quotations from Puškin's works refer to the seventeen-volume edition published by the Academy of Science of the U.S.S.R., M.-L., 1937-1959. When necessary, the lines are indicated in parentheses.

Footnotes

1. See the reference to the reviews in A. G. Gukasova, *Boldinskij period v tvorčestve A. S. Puškina,* M., 1973, p. 151.
2. On A. Grigoriev's theory see S. G. Bočarov, *Poetika, Puškina,* M., 1974, pp. 132-139.
3. V. V. Vinogradov, *Stil' Puškina,* M., 1941, p. 536.
4. See: *Puškin, Itogi i problemy izučenija,* M., 1966, p. 483.
5. A. G. Gukasova, op. cit., p. 201.
6. V. S. Uzin, *O povestjax Belkina,* Akvilon, 1924, p. 6.
7. A. G. Gukasova, op. cit., p. 203.
8. S. S. Bočarov, op. cit., p. 140.
9. Jan M. Meijer, "The Sixth Tale of Belkin," in *The Tales of Belkin by A. S. Puškin,* Essays by Jan van der Eng, A. G. F. Van Holk, Jan M. Meijer, Mouton, 1968, pp. 109-134.
10. Ibid., p. 114.
11. Ibid., p. 115.
12. Ibid., p. 114.
13. S. G. Bočarov, op. cit., p. 147; V. V. Vinogradov, op. cit., p. 538.
14. S. G. Bočarov, op. cit., p. 132.
15. Ibid., p. 139.
16. Ibid., p. 140; V. V. Vinogradov, op. cit., p. 541.
17. S. G. Bočarov, op. cit., p. 153.
18. A. Kodjak, "Šifr Puškina," *The New Review,* N.Y., 1970, No. 101, pp. 80-94.
19. D. Jakubovič, "Predislovie k 'Povestjam Belkina' i povestvovatel'nye priemy Val'ter Skotta," *Puškin v mirovoj literature,* L., 1926.

PART I

DECODING

Chapter 1

BELKIN'S BIOGRAPHY

The sixth tale in Puškin's cycle of short stories has a complex plot with two major subjects—Belkin's biography and the history of the publication of his five stories by the fictional editor, A.P.

The major source of biographical information about Belkin is a letter attributed to his neighbor, the owner of the Nenaradovo estate, written to the editor, A.P., and published by the latter in his foreword to Belkin's *Tales*. Prior to citing the full text of this letter, the editor, A.P., states:

> We are printing it without any changes or footnotes, as a precious monument to a noble manner of thinking and a touching friendship and, at the same time, as a very satisfactory biographical account.[1]

Despite the editor's assertion to the contrary, he makes significant changes in the letter: he omits one anecdote about Belkin and supplements the letter with two footnotes. Both footnotes would glide by unnoticed were it not for the previous statement that there would be no changes in or coments on the letter. Evidently Puškin introduced this discrepancy between the editor's promise and the following text with the aim of attracting the reader's attention to the notes.

The second footnote, especially important for this study, reads as follows:

> Indeed, in Mr. Belkin's manuscript there is an inscription in the author's hand above each tale: "heard by me from such-and-such a person" (rank or title and initials of first name and surname). We extract them for the curious researchers: "The Stationmaster" was told to him by Titular Counsellor A.G.N.; "The Shot" by Lieutenant Colonel I.L.P.; "The Undertaker" by shop assistant B.V.; "The Snowstorm" and "Mistress into Maid" by demoiselle K.I.T.[2]

In the second sentence, "We extract them for the curious researchers," Puškin compels the reader, who must turn into a "researcher," to examine why the note was added. Puškin, however, cleverly misleads the "curious researcher." It appears at first glance that the initials of the narrators and the scant information supplied about them will provide the point of departure for any investigations, but in fact this proves to be incorrect. The key lies not in the initials of the four narrators but in the order in which the tales appear in the footnote. Puškin uses the phrase, "we extract," for a specific reason—to convey the fact that the editor, A.P., is enumerating the tales in the order in which they appear in Belkin's manuscript. Belkin, however, had not arranged them in the order that the editor, A.P., considered acceptable for publication.[3]

Puškin might logically be expected to repeat either the sequence in which the tales were published or, through an oversight perhaps, that in which he himself wrote them, but as the footnote shows, he did neither. One is thereby confronted with two different arrangements of the tales: 1) the order of their publication and 2) the sequence in the editor's footnote (i.e. the order in which Belkin presumably wrote them):

	1		2
a)	"The Shot"	a)	"The Stationmaster"
b)	"The Snowstorm"	b)	"The Shot"
c)	"The Undertaker"	c)	"The Undertaker"
d)	"The Stationmaster"	d)	"The Snowstorm"
e)	"Mistress into Maid"	e)	"Mistress into Maid."

The fact that the tales were reshuffled makes it necessary to examine the role of the fictional editor, A.P., in depth. This examination must lead the researcher to question why the editor changed the sequence of the tales and, furthermore, whether he did so because the cycle would have made a different impression had it been published according to Belkin's plan. Finally, the personalities of I.P. Belkin and the editor, A.P., must be reexamined.

The above observations resulted in this researcher's examination of every detail in the foreword in an attempt to disclose other indications of a cipher beneath which additional facts might lie hidden. Indeed, the concentration of concealed information within this first part of the cycle proves to be astounding. There is a whole series of coded data here which relate either to Belkin himself or to the history of the publication of his tales.

For greater clarity all details in the foreword relevant to the present analysis will be listed. The interrelationship of the individual details will be indicated by cross-references so that the reader can see the entire system of signs at once. Each paragraph will be marked by a Roman numeral, and important points will be italicized and marked by Arabic numbers. The editor's footnotes follow the particular paragraph to which they pertain. The points referred to by Arabic numbers are only briefly commented upon to pose the problems and establish their interrelationship. A more extensive analysis follows after the entire system of signs in the foreword has been established.

I

From the Editor

Having undertaken the struggle to publish the tales of   (1)
I. P. Belkin, herewith presented to the public, we wished
to preface them with a brief account of the life of the
late author and thereby to satisfy in part the justifiable
curiosity of lovers of the literature of our fatherland.
To this end we turned to Marja Alekseevna Trafilina,   (2)
closest relative and heiress of Ivan Petrovič Belkin; but,
unfortunately, she could not furnish any information
whatsoever about him, for she was never even acquainted
with the deceased. *She advised us in this matter to con-*   (3)
*tact a certain worthy gentleman, a former friend of Ivan
Petrovič.* We followed this advice and received the following satisfactory reply to our letter. *We are printing*   (4)
it without any changes or footnotes as a precious monument to a noble manner of thinking and a touching friendship and, at the same time, as a perfectly satisfactory biographical account.

(1)   What is the significance of the phrase, "Having undertaken the struggle (*"vzjavšis' xlopotat'* ")?
(2)   How did the editor learn the name and address of M. A. Travilina?
(3)   From whom did the editor receive the manuscript, since neither Belkin's closest relative nor his neighbor delivered it to A.P.?
(4)   What is the reason for the editor's promise, which he breaks shortly afterwards (cf. points 19, 24)?

II

Most Honored Sir***!
    Your esteemed letter *of the 15th of this month I had*   (5)
the honor to receive on the 23rd of the same month. In
this letter you expressed your desire to secure detailed information regarding the *dates of birth and death, the mil-*   (6)
itary service, the family circumstances, as well as the oc-

cupations and the disposition of the late Ivan Petrovič Belkin, my sincere late friend and neighbor by estates. I take great pleasure in complying with your request, and I am here setting forth to you, most honored Sir, *all that I can remember from our talks* and also from my own   (7)
observations.

(5)   How could the neighbor have answered the editor's letter on November 16, if he did not receive it until the 23rd (cf. points 9 and 31)?

(6)   There is a discrepancy between the neighbor's response to the editor's questions about Belkin and the list of items included in his reply (cf. point 29).

(7)   The neighbor's claim that he has also included in his description of Belkin information gathered from their conversations is suspect, since the neighbor includes no details about Belkin's military career.

III

Ivan Petrovič Belkin was born of honorable and noble parents in the year 1798 in the village of Gorjuxino. *His late father, Second Major Petr Ivanovič Belkin,* was   (8)
married to the demoiselle Pelageja Gavrilovna, *née* Trafilina. He was not a wealthy man but was moderate and extremely shrewd in business matters. His son received his elementary education from the village church reader. It was apparently to this revered man that he owed his love of reading and studying Russian literature. *In 1815 he*   (9)
enlisted in a Jäger infantry regiment (I don't recall the   (10)
number), in which he remained right up until 1823.   (11)
The deaths of his parents, which occurred almost simul-   (12)
taneously, *compelled him to resign his commission,* re-   (13)
tire, and settle in the village of Gorjuxino, his family estate.

(8)   If the neighbor's memory of Belkin's father's rank is so precise, why does he fail to mention Belkin's own rank upon retirement (cf. point 13)?

(9)   These dates, whose last two respective digits repeat the dates of the editor's letter and its receipt by the neighbor, arouse the curiosity of the careful reader (cf. points 5 and 31).

(10)   The neighbor's claim of a slip of memory is suspect considering his otherwise accurate recollections (cf. points 6, 8 and 29).

(11)   Why does the neighbor disguise the year of Belkin's retirement by this rather circuitous choice of phrasing (cf. points 6 and 29)?

(12)   Is this the real reason for Belkin's retirement (cf. points 14, 16, 21; also 6 and 29)?

(13)   The neighbor again fails to mention Belkin's rank (cf. point 8; also point 6 and 10, 11, 12, 29).

IV

After assuming the management of his estate, Ivan Petrovič soon began to neglect the household affairs (because of his inexperience and softheartedness) and relaxed the strict order established by his late parent. Having dismissed his industrious and efficient village elder with whom his peasants (as is their habit) were dissatisfied, he entrusted the management of the estate to his old housekeeper, who had gained his confidence through her ability to tell stories. This stupid old woman had never been able to distinguish a twenty-five-ruble from a fifty-ruble note; she was a godmother to the children of all the peasants, and so the latter were not in fear of her at all; the village elder elected by them indulged them to such an extent, acting in league with them in cheating their master, that *Ivan Petrovič was forced to abolish the system of corvée and to introduce an extremely moderate quit-rent; even then the peasants, taking advantage of his weakness, wheedled all sorts of excessive favors out of him for the first year, and in the following years they paid more than two-thirds of the quit-rent in nuts, cranberries, and the like; and even here there were arrears.* (14)

(15)

(14)   If Belkin neglected his household affairs, what was the real reason for his retirement and his return to his estate (cf. points 12, 16 and 21)?

(15)   Were Belkin's managerial changes an attempt to liberate *de facto* the serfs, to make them economically independent (cf. point 17)?

V

As a friend of Ivan Petrovič's late parent, I *considered*   (16)
it my duty to offer my advice to the son too and re-
peatedly offered to restore the order which he had al-
lowed to fall into decay. For this purpose, having arrived
one day at his estate, I demanded the account books, sum-
moned that swindler of a village elder to come to me,
and began to inspect them in the presence of Ivan Petrovič. At first the young landowner followed my actions with the greatest attention and diligence; but when
it appeared from the accounts that during the last two
years the number of peasants had increased, while the
amount of poultry and cattle had appreciably diminished,
Ivan Petrovič felt satisfied with this initial information and
no longer listened to me. At the very minute when I had
reduced that swindler of a village elder to extreme embarrassment with my investigation and *stern interrogation*   (17)
and had silenced him completely, to my extreme vexation
I heard Ivan Petrovič snoring loudly in his chair. Thereafter I ceased to interfere in his actions regarding the
management of his estate and entrusted his affairs (as he
himself did) to the care of the Almighty.

(16)   If the neighbor was willing to involve himself in Belkin's
managerial affairs, why did Belkin have to retire (cf.
points 12, 14 and 21)?

(17)   Could anyone possibly fall asleep sitting on a chair in the
same room in which the neighbor conducted his interrogation (cf. point 15)?

VI

This matter did not disturb our friendly relations in any
way, however; for, commiserating as I did with his weakness and that ruinous neglect common to our young
noblemen, I sincerely liked Ivan Petrovič; indeed, it would
have been impossible not to be fond of so gentle and
honest a young man. On his part, Ivan Petrovič showed
respect for my years and was warmly attached to me.
Until his very end he saw me almost daily, valuing my   (18)
simple conversation, although in habits, manner of think-
ing, and disposition we had very little in common for
the most part.

(18)   Why does the neighbor claim friendship with Belkin while stressing their utter incompatibility (cf. point 28)?

VII

Ivan Petrovič lived in the most moderate fashion and avoided excess of any sort; I never had occasion to see him tipsy (which in our parts may be considered an unheard-of miracle); he had a great weakness for the female sex, but in fact was as bashful as a girl.[1]

---

1. *An anecdote follows which we are not printing, as we consider it superfluous; however, we assure the reader that it contains nothing prejudicial to the memory of Ivan Petrovič Belkin.*   (19)

(19)   Why does the editor footnote the neighbor's letter after promising not to do so (cf. points 4 and 24)?

VIII

Besides the tales which you mention in your letter, Ivan (20) *Petrovič left a great number of manuscripts, some of which I have in my possession, some of which his housekeeper used for various domestic purposes. Thus, last winter she sealed up all the windows in her wing with the first part of a novel which he did not complete. It seems* (21) *that the tales mentioned above were his first effort. As* (22) *Ivan Petrovič said, they are for the most part, true stories which he had heard from various people.[2] The characters' names, however, were almost all invented by him, while names of the hamlets and villages were borrowed from our district for which reason my own village is mentioned* (23) *somewhere.* This came about not through any evil intention, but solely from lack of imagination.

---

2. *Indeed, in Mr. Belkin's manuscript there is an inscription in* (24) *the author's hand above each tale: "heard by me from such-and-such a person" (rank or title and initials of first name and surname). We extract them for the curious researchers: "The Sta-* (25) *tionmaster" was told to him by Titular Counselor A.G.N., "The* (26) *Shot" by Lieutenant Colonel I.L.P., "The Undertaker" by shop assistant B.V., "The Snowstorm" and "Mistress into Maid" by demoiselle K.I.T.*

(20)   Had Belkin made no arrangements for his manuscripts before his death (cf. point 27)?

(21)   In light of the neighbor's obvious willingness to concern
       himself with Belkin's estate even after his death, one must
       question again the reason for Belkin's retirement (cf. points
       12, 14 and 16).
(22)   Why were only Belkin's first literary attempts sent for pub-
       lication, while subsequent works remained on his estate?
(23)   Why does the neighbor volunteer this information?
(24)   For the second time the editor adds a footnote, thus break-
       ing his promise (cf. 4 and 19).
(25)   Why does A.P. address, not his readers in general, but "curi-
       ous researchers"?
(26)   Why does the editor change the sequence of the tales when
       he publishes them?

IX

In the autumn of 1828 Ivan Petrovič caught a chill which   (27)
led to a high fever, and he died, despite the tireless efforts
of our local doctor, a man of great skill, particularly in
the treatment of chronic disease, such as corns and the
like. *Ivan Petrovič died in my arms in the thirtieth year*   (28)
of his life and was buried next to his parents in the grave-
yard of the village of Gorjuxino.

(27)   Since Belkin's death was not sudden, why did he fail to
       make some provision for his manuscripts (cf. point 20)?
(28)   Why did Belkin die in the arms of a man with whom he had
       nothing in common (cf. point 18)?

X

Ivan Petrovič was of medium height, had grey eyes, light
brown hair, and a straight nose; his face was lean and of
light complexion.

XI

And that, most honored Sir, is everything that I have been
able to recall *concerning the manner of life, occupa-*   (29)
tions, disposition and appearance of my late neighbor and
friend. However, if you should see fit to make use of any
part of my letter, I would ask you most respectfully to
refrain from mentioning my name; for *as much as I like*   (30)

authors and greatly respect them, I consider it super-
fluous, and at my age, unfitting to embark on this call-
ing. With my sincere respects, etc.

(29)   Why does the neighbor omit Belkin's military service in
       the list of his replies to the editor's query (cf. points 6,
       also 10, 11, 12, and 13)?
(30)   Why does the neighbor take care to disassociate himself
       from "authors," since the information he provides about
       Belkin presumably would not be construed as fiction?

XII

1830. *November 16.*   (31)
Village of Nenaradovo

(31)   How can the neighbor reply on November 16 to a letter
       that he did not receive until November 23 (cf. point 5)?

XIII

Considering it our duty to respect the wish of our late
author's esteemed friend, we convey our deepest gratitude
to him for the information he has provided us, and we
trust that our public will appreciate its sincerity and
goodness.

XIV

A.P.   (32) (33)

(32)   Why are the initials of the editor the same as Puškin's?
(33)   Why is the neighbor's letter addressed to *** instead of
       to A.P.? Are A.P. and the editor not identical?

From all appearances the neighbor is fond of precision, as the beginning of his letter shows: "Your esteemed letter of the 15th of this month
I had the honor to receive on the 23rd of the same month . . ." (II, 5).[4]
The name of the month appears only at the end of the letter: "1830. November 16" (XII). There is a striking contradiction here: the neighbor
replies to the editor's letter of November 16, that is, on the day after the
editor wrote his letter (November 15) and seven days before the neighbor supposedly received it (November 23). The "curious researcher"
must respond to the error; comparing the dates again, he registers the
numbers 15, 23, 16. In the second paragraph of the letter the first two
pairs of digits are repeated in the same sequence: "In 1815 he [Belkin]

enlisted in a Jäger infantry regiment (I don't recall the number), in which he remained right up until 1823" (III, 9, 10, 11). The last two digits of these dates repeat the numbers 15 and 23. Once the attention of the researcher has been drawn to those numbers through Puškin's insertion of an error in dating the letters, one then begins to read more carefully. On closer inspection, however, the coincidence of the twenty-threes is only an apparent one, for Belkin, in fact, retired not in 1823 but at the end of 1822 (". . . in which he remained right up until 1823") (III, 11). Here Puškin could have used one of two Russian expressions of time, *do 1823 goda,* which could include a part of 1823, or *do samogo 1823 goda,* meaning right up until 1823 but not including it. Puškin used the latter expression. This sentence is worded differently in the first draft which reads as follows: "In 1818 he graduated and enlisted as an officer in the Selenginsk infantry regiment, in which he served through 1822."[5] Apparently Puškin originally intended to have Belkin retire in 1822 but felt it unwise to state the year outright; thus, he replaced the year 1822 with the phrase, "right up until 1823," thereby disguising the actual year of retirement. This phrase might have escaped the attention of the "curious researcher" had the inconsistency in the dates of the letters and the coincidence of the years not caught his eye.

Puškin uses false motivation extensively throughout the foreword. The story of Belkin's so-called retirement is a case in point. Belkin leaves the Jäger infantry regiment allegedly because of the death of his parents (II, 12), but this circumstance in itself would scarcely justify his retirement. The necessity of managing the estate might have induced him to return to his remote province, but the letter indicates that he did not come to Gorjuxino with the intention of exploiting the land at all (IV, 14). After his parents died, Belkin easily could have entrusted his affairs to the village elder under the supervision of the Nenaradovo neighbor whose willingness to manage the estate was apparent even after Belkin's death; the neighbor continued to pay visits to Gorjuxino and even knew with which part of Belkin's novel the housekeeper sealed up her windows for the winter (VIII, 21). Domestic considerations clearly did not provide the incentive for Belkin's retirement. It was not due to marriage, for Belkin died a bachelor. He might have lost at gambling previously, but this was not like him; on the contrary, his finances indicate that he had no debts of honor. He could have retired owing to quarreling or dueling, as Silvio did in "The Shot," but that would have contradicted his nature. The neighbor, then, provides a spurious reason for Belkin's retirement and is silent about the conditions surrounding it.

Omissions and zero signs constitute yet another type of cipher. As mentioned above, Belkin's neighbor is a man of precision. Though not called upon to do so, he enters the date of the editor's letter as well as the date on which he received it, recalls the essential dates in Belkin's life and remembers the maiden name of Belkin's mother and the rank of his father (III, 8). But in the midst of all his deliberate precision and accuracy, the neighbor "forgets" a very important detail: "In 1815 he enlisted in a Jäger infantry regiment (I don't recall the number), in which he remained right up until 1823" (III, 10). The neighbor is aware that it was a Jäger infantry regiment, notes the year Belkin entered it and knows that Belkin was not transferred from this regiment but served there until his retirement. Nevertheless, the neighbor cannot recall the number of the regiment, though his mention of it is testimony to the fact that he considers it important. His silence on this subject is part of an entire code which veils Belkin's army career. One naturally expects to find Belkin's specific rank upon retirement mentioned in the letter, particularly in view of the fact that the neighbor notes that Belkin's father was a second major (III, 8). Indeed a mysterious cloud obscures Ivan Petrovič's career in the service—the most important achievement of a nobleman of the time.

The lack of information on this point may seem not at all suspicious to the general reader. The neighbor was not a fellow officer of Belkin's. While Belkin was with his regiment, his neighbor was living at home in the country and, therefore, could not have known about Ivan Petrovič's military life. The neighbor may well have considered it uninteresting to the editor. Puškin, however, precludes such objections. In addition to other requests, the editor specifically asks for information concerning the military career of Ivan Petrovič, as the neighbor himself states: ". . . you expressed your desire to secure detailed information regarding . . . the military service . . . of the late Ivan Petrovič Belkin . . ." (II, 6). Though the neighbor replies fully to all the other questions posed by the editor, he evades Belkin's service evidently intentionally, since it is inconceivable that he did not hear about Belkin's army career in his daily encounters with him unless Belkin himself had reason to avoid the subject. The neighbor certainly draws upon Belkin's recollections to provide other biographical information. He writes to A.P.: ". . . I am here setting forth to you, most honored Sir, all that I can remember from our talks . . ." (II, 7). But the neighbor fails to comment on that topic of conversation that would have been of most interest to those remaining in the backwoods—Belkin's life in the regiment. The omissions in the neighbor's letter coupled with the aforementioned inconsistencies ultimately lead to two questions: Why did Belkin retire, and why did he retire without being promoted?

The mystery surrounding Belkin's military service again surfaces in the concluding paragraph of the letter wherein the neighbor summarizes all that he has just said about Belkin: "And that, most honored Sir, is everything that I have been able to recall concerning the manner of life, occupations, disposition and appearance of my late neighbor and friend" (XI, 29). The editor, however, requested information on the dates of Belkin's birth and death, his military service, family circumstances, his occupations, and his character (II, 6). Why does the neighbor in his summary omit any reference to Belkin's military service? The point begs for investigation, for the neighbor has failed to include in Belkin's biography the exact location of his regiment, which could have been ascertained from its number, and the year of, his reason for, and rank upon retirement. The withholding of only the last two details might well have been due to personal failures that Belkin was reluctant to relate to his neighbor. The omission of the location of his regiment coupled with the coding of the year of his retirement is due, however, not to Belkin's personal circumstances in the service (which could occur at any time in any regiment) but, most likely, rather to certain events of a public nature that occurred at a specific time and place—in 1822 in one of the Jäger infantry regiments.

As mentioned above, Puškin's first draft contains substantially more information on Belkin's military service and states definitely that Belkin retired in 1822.[6] According to the second draft, he served in the Selenginsk regiment and retired with the rank of lieutenant.[7] Puškin was aware of the existence of this regiment from the time of his exile in Kišinev, where many liberal officers of the Second Army were stationed. Puškin's friend, I. P. Liprandi, writes the following:

> I spent three of four evenings, and sometimes even more, at home. My constant visitors were: Oxotnikov; the Major, head of the Division's Lancaster School-V. F. Raevskij; Major Janovskij of the Kamchatka regimen—a remarkably original man whose adventures during French captivity after the Austerlitz battle were not devoid of interest; Lieutenant Taušev of the Sixteenth Division, a well-educated young man from Kazan University; Major Gaevskij, transferred out of the Guard into the Selenginsk regiment as a result of the Semenov regiment affair[8] and appointed here by Orlov as head of the training battalion. . . .[9]

Puškin frequently visited Liprandi and, of course, knew all these officers as well as the reason for Gaevskij's transfer to the Selenginsk regiment. Puškin may well have planned to include Belkin at these gatherings. Indeed in the first and second drafts of the foreword Belkin belonged to the same Selenginsk regiment in which one of the participants in the uprising of the Semenov regiment served. In the final edition of the tales, however, Puškin replaced the Selenginsk regiment with the Jäger infantry regiment whose number the neighbor has allegedly forgotten. Nevertheless, the fact that Belkin served in southern Russia and in all probability in Kišinev is indicated by many signs dispersed throughout his tales.

L. Grossman has established that Silvio, the protagonist of "The Shot," is modeled after Puškin's friend in Kišinev, Lieutenant Colonel I. P. Liprandi,[10] whose initials and rank are also reflected in the meager information provided in the editor's footnote about the narrator of the same story. Obviously Kišinev and the group of liberal officers were on Puškin's mind while he was writing *The Tales of Belkin*. It was not a precise documentary picture of Kišinev in the early 1820's that Puškin was striving for but rather pointed details that would remind the informed reader of familiar facts and thus place Puškin's work in the proper historical perspective. In "The Shot," for example, Puškin does not portray Liprandi but introduces some traces of his character in Silvio and at the same time links another character, Lieutenant Colonel I.L.P., the narrator, to Liprandi by means of their rank and initials. Liprandi appears in two different functions—first as a mysterious person of exceptional experience and background (Silvio) and second as a simple officer fascinated by stories of duels (the narrator, I.L.P.).

Puškin spent almost three years in Kišinev. During this time he had several opportunities to travel throughout southern Russia. He must have been well acquainted with the surrounding towns not unlike Tul'čin, where the headquarters of the Second Army were located and where most of the meetings of the southern branch of the Decembrists were held. A description of Tul'čin appears in the memoirs of N. V. Basargin, who served under General Kiselev in 1822:

> Tulčino, a little Polish town that belonged then to Count Mečislav Potockij, was populated by Jews and Polish nobility. Aside from the military and the officials at general headquarters there was no society.[11]

The similarity between this passage and the introduction to "The Shot" is striking:

> We were stationed in the small town of ***. The life of an army officer is known to all. In the morning, drill, riding school; dinner at the Regiment Commander's or in a Jewish inn; in the evening, drinks and cards. In *** there was not a single house open to us

nor one marriageable girl; we gathered in each others' rooms, where there was nothing to look at except our own uniforms.[12]

Though the two descriptions are similar, this in itself does not constitute proof that Puškin had Tul'čin in mind, since there were many such southern towns at that time. The details in Puškin's obviously coded stories must be examined in their totality, for individually they do not provide the key to the hidden meaning. Only Puškin's contemporaries could understand the cipher, and it was for them that the superficial, quotidian details took on the greatest meaning. Thus the similarities between Tul'čin and the town where Silvio lives must be considered in conjunction with certain other signs in the entire cycle.

In Kišinev, Puškin became acquainted with Alexander Ypsilanti, who at that time was preparing the Greek rebellion against Turkish rule, about which Puškin wrote some historic notes in French and a short story, "Kirdžali," in 1834. The epilogue of "The Shot," by mentioning Ypsilanti, thus indirectly recalls Kišinev, where the news of his rebellion had undoubtedly spread. The formulation of the narrator, I.L.P's last statement is puzzling: "They say that Silvio during the rebellion of Alexander Ypsilanti commanded a detachment of heterists and was killed in the battle of Skuljany."[13] This remark implies a change in I.L.P.'s life style: after his retirement he has found himself in the backwoods totally isolated from the outside world and only a few years later, 1821-1825, has already received the news of Silvio's death in a hopeless battle from which only a few survivors escaped. The question that follows from this observation is whether the epilogue should be ascribed to I.L.P., who, as Grossman has already pointed out, suggests by his rank and initials I. P. Liprandi, or whether the epilogue should be regarded as Belkin's addition to the story. In either case, of course, the Kišinev setting remains the only possible one for "The Shot," since no matter to whom the epilogue is ascribed, the details of Silvio's death set the story in southern Russia.

From Puškin's experience in the South one can see further in "The Undertaker." On May 4, 1821, during Puškin's stay in Kišinev, he was admitted to the Ovidis Masonic Lodge. Masonic Lodges, although quite numerous in Russia during the reign of Alexander I, were limited almost exclusively to the nobility or wealthy class. It is rather difficult to expect B.V., the narrator of "The Undertaker," a *prikazčik*, a shopkeeper or estate manager obviously of humble origin, for he lacks an initial for a patronymic, to be a member of a Masonic Lodge. In "The Undertaker," however, there is the mention of three Masonic knocks on the door, a detail which like the references to Shakespeare and Sir Walter Scott should be attributed to Belkin rather than to the narrator, B.V.

Puškin's southern experiences may be traced as well in "Mistress into Maid," in which Alexej, after giving Akulina several successful reading lessons, exclaims: "It's a miracle. . . . Our system of learning works better than the Lancaster system."[14] According to the editor's footnote, the narrator of this story, as well as of "The Snowstorm," is a young lady, K.I.T. It would be presumptuous to expect her to know about the Lancaster system of education or to ascribe to her a passage from "The Snowstorm" dealing with Russian women:

> The women, the Russian women, were beyond comparison in those days. Their usual coldness vanished. Their enthusiasm was truly intoxicating when, welcoming the conquerors, *they cried "hurrah" and threw their caps into the air.* What officer of that time will not confess that he is indebted to the Russian women for his best and most precious reward . . . ?[15]

Besides the quotation from Griboedov's *Woe from Wit* which would hardly have been accessible to a young lady, particularly as at that time it was still unpublished, the entire passage reflects rather a man's point of view and thus, along with the reference to the Lancaster system in "Mistress into Maid," should be ascribed to Belkin rather than to the young, provincial lady, K.I.T. Puškin must have been well acquainted with the Lancaster system of education from his years spent in Kišinev. In the passage quoted above, Liprandi mentions Major V. F. Raevskij, who supervised the Lancaster schools for soldiers of the 16th Infantry Division. One of the reasons for Raevskij's arrest on February 6, 1822, was his political propagandizing in these schools. From Raevskij's memoirs it is clear that Puškin had warned him of arrest.[16] I. Puščin's memoirs note that Puškin recalled Major Raevskij three years later during Puščin's visit to Mixajlovskoe.[17] According to Liprandi, Puškin and Major Raevskij quite frequently engaged in heated debates.[18] Thus Raevskij and his Lancaster schools in the 16th Infantry Division must have been well known to the small circle of officers to which Puškin belonged.

The 16th Infantry Division is also linked with the Lancaster system of education through the commander, General M. F. Orlov, a notorious promulgator of the system. Because of Orlov's liberal treatment of privates the 16th Division became famous and was referred to as *orlovščina.* Orlov's and Raevskij's Lancaster schools were one of the reasons for this notoriety.[19]

In view of all these circumstances the Lancaster system of education referred to with admiration in one of Belkin's tales clearly reinforces the system of signs establishing Kišinev as the place where Belkin was stationed and his military service as the only possible period in his life

when he could have been exposed to such ideas. Assuming that Belkin
was stationed in Kišinev and knowing that Puškin originally placed Belkin
in the Selenginsk regiment, one must only discover whether there was
a Jäger infantry regiment well known to Puškin's circle and stationed in
the Kišinev region. This question leads to the 32nd Infantry Jäger Regiment in which Major V. F. Raevskij served and which was part of the
famous 16th Infantry Division of General M. F. Orlov. If Belkin's neighbor had revealed the number of the regiment, Belkin's biography would
have been immediately apparent. The precise number of the regiment
had to be omitted by the neighbor in order that he might portray Belkin
as a colorless and mediocre figure.

For Puškin's knowledgeable contemporaries the conspicuous omission of the number of Belkin's regiment could have been sufficient indica-
tion that it was the 32nd Jäger Regiment of the 16th Infantry Division.
Puškin, however, left a clue to his code for less knowledgeable readers
—the sequence of numbers relating to the precise date of Belkin's retirement. In the neighbor's letter two numerical sequences are established:
1815 and 1823; 15, 23, and 16. Both sequences are mutilated: in the first
there is an omission exposed by the excuse, "I don't recall the number"
(III, 10), and in the second the sequence of the dates contradicts the order
in which the events had to occur, namely the date of the neighbor's response (XII, 31).

The question is how or why does the otherwise rather meticulous
neighbor make a mistake in dating his letter? Why does he write November 16 instead of perhaps 26? Either the neighbor knows the numbers of Belkin's regiment and division but decides to withhold the information (this version is accepted in this analysis) or honestly fails to
recollect the number of the regiment. In any case, both numbers—32 and
16—could easily cross the neighbor's mind. Thus one may assume that
Puškin imagined the neighbor writing the letter with one of the numbers
in mind and that it slipped into the date at the end of the letter. Within
Puškin's system of signs leading the reader to Kišinev the connection
between the Jäger Infantry regiment, the number of which is conspicuously omitted, and the number sixteen, conspicuously misplaced at
the end of the letter, are perfectly in order. An analogical situation has
already been established in "The Shot" in which two characters in two
different ways suggest I. P. Liprandi. The researcher's assumption that
Belkin served in the 32nd Jäger Infantry regiment in the 16th Infantry
division becomes a conviction when other details mysteriously omitted
in his biography such as the year, his rank, and the reason for his retirement are examined.

Any of Puškin's contemporaries who lived in Kišinev in 1822 or who were in close contact with an eyewitness of those events would know that in that year there was a wave of forced retirements. After the arrest of Major V. F. Raevskij on February 6, 1822, I. P. Liprandi retired under strange circumstances on November 11, 1822;[20] General Orlov's aide-de-camp Captain K. A. Oxotnikov was forced into retirement "for family reasons" and left his detachment on April 11, 1822;[21] Major General P. S. Puščin, the founder of the Masonic Lodge, "Ovid," to which Puškin also belonged, was forced into retirement on March 30, 1822;[22] and Major General M. A. Fonvizin retired on December 25, 1822.[23] In the same year Colonel A. G. Nepenin also retired;[24] and the next year, on April 18, Major General M. F. Orlov, Commander of the 16th Infantry division, was forced out of his post.[25] Thus, Belkin's retirement in 1822 for no obvious reason clearly reflects the situation in the 16th Division and the 32nd Jäger regiment in Kišinev. Furthermore, the omission of Belkin's rank implies that he also may have been forced to retire without promotion—i.e., almost dishonorably discharged[26] (II, 13).

In light of the above, another detail in the neighbor's letter acquires new interest: "The deaths of his parents, which occurred almost simultaneously, compelled him to resign his commission and retire . . ," (II, 12). It has already been shown that this reason for retirement is hardly convincing, since Belkin would not have had to return to manage his estate. However, the deaths of both his parents so close together in 1822 may arouse the suspicion that the news of their son's involvement in a conspiracy against the government contributed to their demise.

Belkin's parents must have been relatively young when they died, since their son at that time was only twenty-four years old. Belkin's father was presumably of the same generation as his neighbor who seems to be in good health in 1830. No epidemic or any kind of accident is mentioned in the letter as a cause of their almost simultaneous deaths. The neighbor's silence on this point contrasts so markedly with the rest of his letter in which the causality of every single event without exception is meticulously noted that one cannot help but perceive the lack of detail surrounding this incident as an intentional omission. Their unexplained deaths which the neighbor seizes upon as a pretext for Belkin's retirement thus appear even more suspicious.

A similar situation occurs in the last chapter of Puškin's *The Captain's Daughter*. There the parents of Grinev, after receiving the news of their son's arrest for his alleged participation in Pugačev's uprising, suffer extreme depression. In Grinev's words, "This unexpected blow nearly killed my father. . . . Terrified by his despair, my mother did not dare to cry in his presence. . . ."[27] Such a reaction might also have characterized Belkin's parents' attitude toward their son's dishonor.

Grinev and Belkin's fathers are obviously of the same psychological type
—conservative, military men retired with almost the same rank: Grinev
was a first major; Belkin, a second major. Both Petr Grinev and Ivan
Belkin were the only sons of their parents (Grinev was one of nine
children, but eight of them had died in early childhood.) Thus the situa-
tions are similar indeed: A conservative man with a military background
sees his only son and heir becoming a criminal and a traitor to the crown.
While old Grinev was nearly killed by the news of his son's treason, so
might the old Belkin have broken down and died. Belkin's mother, having buried her husband, could easily have succumbed to her double grief.
Thus the almost simultaneous deaths of Belkin's parents cease to seem
an unimportant coincidence and become a meaningful sign with its
unique place and function in the entire system.

A tiny detail supports this assumption. Speaking about his relationship with Ivan Petrovič Belkin, the neighbor writes: "I sincerely liked
Ivan Petrovič; indeed, it would have been impossible not to be fond of
so gentle and honest a young man" (VI). The epithet "*čestnyj*" as used
by the neighbor means honorable and loyal. Since Belkin was a nobleman,
under normal circumstances there would have been no need to defend
his honor and loyalty unless some suspicion of the opposite existed. The
neighbor's reference to honesty would seem to be a slip of the tongue.
With great subtlety Puškin pictures the neighbor as a friend of Belkin's
father, aware of Belkin's involvement in a political conspiracy and a wit-
ness to the tragic events affecting Belkin's family who was desperately
trying to protect the honor of his late friend, Second Major Petr Ivanovič
Belkin.

> At this point it is appropriate to recall the laments of the old Grinev:
> What! he repeated, beside himself. My son is an accomplice of
> Pugačov! Good God, what have I lived to see! The Empress
> spares him from execution! Does that make it any better for me?
> It is not the execution that is horrifying. My great-great-grandfather
> died on a scafforld defending what was sacred in his conscience; my
> father was persecuted with Volynskij and Xruščev. But for a
> nobleman to betray his oath of allegiance and join brigands, mur-
> derers and fugitive serfs! . . . Shame and disgrace to our name! . . .[28]

It is the honor of Belkin's name that the neighbor was so carefully
protecting in his letter to A.P., who in turn, in all probability having understood the neighbor's intentions, comments on his letter in a way that
remains inexplicable unless the tragic reality is revealed: "We are printing it . . . as a precious monument to a noble manner of thinking and a

touching friendship and, at the same time, as a perfectly satisfactory biographical account." (I) this hyperbolic praise becomes appropriate in light of the above.

On the basis of all these data Belkin's biography would seem to reflect the fate of a member of the Kišinev group of Decembrists. In 1830 circumstances did not require that Puškin code Belkin's military career in detail, since they did not allow Puškin to connect his hero irrefutably with the southern branch of the Decembrists. Allusion was sufficient for Puškin's need. Indeed, allusion was the sole artistic device by which the events and individuals associated with the Decembrist uprising could be mentioned publicly at that time. However, the allusions and coded details likely were understood by those who knew of the situation in Kišinev.

The second part of Belkin's biography—his life in Gorjuxino—acquires a new flavor when perceived in the light of Belkin's affiliation with the southern branch of the Decembrists. It is Belkin's managerial philosophy that must be reevaluated. The neighbor in his letter laments bitterly Belkin's inefficiency and soft-heartedness (IV). The neighbor repeatedly offered his advice to Belkin (IV) but in vain. Indeed, Belkin, otherwise amenable, showed a remarkable resistance to all of the neighbor's attempts to "restore the order" which was established by Belkin's father. The difference between the old (the father's) and the new (the son's) management was radical—Ivan Petrovič replaced the corvée by a ridiculously liberal quit-rent. In other words, he refused to profit from the labor of his serfs and made them, if not legally, at least economically, independent.

The political views of Belkin's neighbor are implied in his letter to the editor. It is understandable why Belkin pretended to be feeble-minded and inefficient in his new role of landowner while dealing with his conservative neighbor. Fortunately, the neighbor's simple-mindedness allowed Belkin to mislead him and to cover his small agrarian reform. This situation, however, easily could have resulted in open conflict during the neighbor's last attempt to establish the old order on Belkin's estate (V). The ambiguity of their relations reaches its peak during the neighbor's tactless intrusion into Belkin's managerial affairs and interrogation of the elder. The neighbor's effort, however, was abortive, for Belkin fell asleep (V, 17).

The description of this scene, however, must attract the attention of the "curious researcher." Three details in their totality are suspicious: first, Belkin's falling asleep exactly when the neighbor triumphs over the village elder; second, Belkin's sleeping during the "stern interrogation" while sitting on a straight chair; and lastly, Belkin's snoring, which could be interpreted as his last resort in this embarrassing situation to interrupt the interrogation of the village elder without offending the neighbor and without professing his liberal philosophy. Consequently, one must include Belkin's snoring in the system of Puškin's code and perceive it as a maneuver rather than as a sign of Belkin's feeble-mindedness.

The two parts of Belkin's biography after decoding are in perfect agreement with each other. His experience in General Orlov's 16th Division among the southern Decembrists led him to managerial reforms on his estate. As in Orlov's Division the privates were treated in an exceptionally humane way, so on Belkin's estate the serfs practically were freed from their economic burden. In order to preclude any suspicion of dangerous liberalism, Belkin used a camouflage: his pretense of eccentricity and his snoring during the interrogation of the village elder.

Camouflage also served Belkin in protecting his main occupation —writing. During the six years that elapsed between his retirement in 1822 and his death in 1828, he produced a considerable number of manuscripts including a novel and a cycle of five short stories, his first literary effort. These five tales reached the editor, A.P., in a mysterious way.

Footnotes

1. P., v. 8, I, p. 59 (13-16).
2. Ibid., p. 61 (35-40).
3. The Russian verb, *vypisyvat'*, means in this context "to extract." The other verbs that could be used here are *spisyvat'*, which would mean simply to copy, not necessarily in the same sequence as the original, or *perepisyvat'*, to rewrite or to make a copy, which would include the entire original text. According to the *Slovar' jazyka Puškina*, M., 1961, Puškin distinguishes among these verbs.

   Thus there is no doubt that the change in the order of the tales, not the identity of the narrators, is the information being conveyed to the "curious researchers." Vinogradov, however, concentrates on the narrators in his comprehensive study, *Stil' Puškina*, in which he analyzes their language in an attempt to distinguish among the styles of the five tales. Unfortunately Vinogradov's analysis does not lead to any significant conclusions. It remains unclear which stylistic features should be ascribed to the narrator and which to Belkin or the editor, A.P. It appears that Vinogradov's most interesting and useful study was based on a mistaken assumption, that Puškin envisioned Belkin as a kind of stenographer who recorded the stories of various narrators so faithfully that even the slightest idiosyncrasy in their styles could be detected in his tales. The fact, however, is that Puškin created Belkin, a writer who based his tales on the anecdotes related to him by different narrators. The stylistic differences detected by Vinogradov in the tales testify to Belkin's own literary experimentation rather than to the distinctive styles of the four narrators.

   See: V. V. Vinogradov, *Stil' Puškina*, Moscow, 1941, pp. 537-579.
4. P., v. 8. I, pp. 59 (18-19). Hereafter all references to the foreword, "From the Editor," are made to the text presented in this chapter; Roman numerals mark paragraphs, and, when necessary, Arabic numerals refer to specific problems.
5. P., v. II, p. 582.
6. Ibid.
7. Ibid., p. 585.

8. In October, 1820, the soldiers of the Semenov Regiment, one of the most elite in the Imperial Guard, rebelled. The rebellion was quickly suppressed; the soldiers were arrested; and the officers were dispersed throughout the army.
9. See: A. S. *Puškin v vospominanijax sovremennikov*, V.I., M., 1974, p. 298.
10. L. Grossman, "Istoričeskij fon 'Vystrela' " in *Cex pera*, M., 1930, pp. 203-235.
11. "Zapiski Nikolaja Vasil'eviča Basargina," in Bartenev: *Devjatnadcatyj vek*, M., 1872, Book I, p. 65.
12. P., v. 8, I, p. 65 (7-11).
13. Ibid., p. 74 (38-40).
14. Ibid., p. 121 (27-29).
15. Ibid., p. 83 (20-25).
16. *A. E. Puškin v vospominanijax sovremennikov*, op. cit., v. I., p. 370.
17. Ibid., p. 108-109.
18. Ibid., pp. 298-299.
19. See: G. Geršenzon, *Molodaja Rossija*, M., 1908, p. 10.
20. See: *Vosstannie Dekazbristov*, Materialy, L., 1925, v. 8, "Alfavit Dekabristov," p. 343.
21. Ibid., p. 370.
22. Ibid., p. 382.
23. Ibid., p. 411.
24. See: *Literaturnoe nasledstvo*, No. 60, p. 58.
25. See: *Vosstanie Dekabristov*, op. cit., p. 369. Also G. Geršenzon op. cit., p. 37. The same facts are described from a conservative point of view by F. F. Vigel' in his memoirs. Referring to the liberal officers in General M. F. Orlov's circle and their discussions, Vigel' writes:

> All of this was said and transpired in broad daylight witnessed by all Bessarabia. The commander of the army corps, Ivan Vasil'evič Sabaneev, an officer of Suvorov's time, who was worshipping this great support of the Russian throne, could not view this with indifference. Over the head of the Chief of Staff and even against his will, Sabanneev reported all of this to Petersburg. Orlov was ordered to leave his command post; Puščin was ordered to retire. Oxotnikov fortunately died, and Raevskij was imprisoned in the Tiraspol' fortress,—thus this affair ended (*A. S. Puškin v vospominanijax sovremennikov*, op. cit., p. 223).

F. Vigel' is inaccurate in the case of Oxotnokov, who was forced to retire, moved to his estate, and died there of tuberculosis in 1824.
26. It was customary to promote an officer upon retirement. The most flagrant example of the violation of this tradition is the case of P. Čaadaev, whom Alexander I because of extreme dissatisfaction with him neglected to promote in 1820.
27. P., v. 8, I, p. 370 (1, 10).
28. Ibid. (3-10).

CHAPTER 2

THE PUBLICATION OF BELKIN'S MANUSCRIPT

The path Belkin's manuscript took to the editor, A.P., and the latter's efforts to publish it comprise the second subject of the sixth tale, the foreword. The facts presented in the first paragraph of the foreword are as follows. The editor, A.P., finds himself in possession of a manuscript with five tales written by the obscure I.P. Belkin. The editor knows nothing about the author but would like to provide the "lovers of the literature of our fatherland" with some information about him. Therefore, having never met Belkin before, he finds in some mysterious way the name and address of Belkin's closest relative and heiress, M. A. Trafilina, and communicates with her. It turns out, however, that she was not even acquainted with her relative, I. P. Belkin. Nevertheless, she knew Belkin's neighbor and directed the editor, A.P., to him. In this way the problem was solved (I, 2, 3).

Although this story, as A.P. presents it, at first seems perfectly plausible, after some reflection it appears unclear how the editor could have gotten in touch with M. A. Trafilina. Of course, she could have been known to the neighbor who after Belkin's death likely assumed responsibility for his property and the legal matters concerning the inheritance of his estate. The neighbor could have known about the close relatives of Belkin's family, since he was a good friend of Belkin's father. The strangest fact, however, is that it was not the neighbor who directed the editor to Trafilina but Trafilina who directed the editor to the neighbor. Thus one must address oneself to the question: From whom did the editor receive the name and address of Trafilina?

The puzzle is accompanied by another mystery: From whom did the editor receive Belkin's manuscript, if, as is apparent from the foreword, he was never in communication with the deceased author of the stories? Belkin's only relative about whom the editor allegedly knew was Trafilina, but as she was not even acquainted with Belkin, she surely could not have sent his manuscript to A.P. The neighbor had possession of Belkin's other manuscripts, but the editor communicated with him only after deciding to publish Belkin's tales. Thus, the neighbor did not send them to A.P. either. Obviously there is a missing link between the editor and Belkin that had to be kept concealed for some important reason.

36

Only two things are certain—that the editor had Belkin's manuscript and that A.P. exchanged letters with Belkin's neighbor after deciding to publish the tales. It is questionable whether the editor communicated with M. A. Trafilina, and thus it is possible that he simply fabricated this contact. The name Trafilina is mentioned in the neighbor's letter (III), and thus A.P. simply could have extracted it.

Thus one may hypothesize that there was someone, perhaps a friend of Belkin, who knew both Belkin and the editor, had previously visited Belkin in Gorjuxino, delivered Belkin's manuscript to the editor, and suggested to A.P. that he contact the neighbor. If for some reason the identity of this intermediary had to remain unknown to the public or the government, the editor was forced to create another version of the story. Thus he could simply take Belkin's mother's maiden name from the neighbor's letter and claim that he had communicated with M.A. Trafilina first. In any case is it likely that the editor would have obtained from a hypothetical friend of Belkin's the name and address of Trafilina, a relative with whom Belkin was not acquainted? This hypothesis will be examined in light of all the other relevant facts that could help to supply the missing link between Belkin and the editor A.P.

Belkin, no doubt, completed his tales by 1825.[1] The neighbor's letter indicates that the remainder of his literary works apparently remained in Gorjuxino and Nenaradovo: "Besides the tales which you mention in your letter, Ivan Petrovič left a great number of manuscripts, some of which I have in my possession, some of which his housekeeper used for various domestic purposes" (VIII, 20). The tales, therefore, were the sole known works of Belkin to appear outside Gorjuxino and Nenaradovo before December 14, 1825.

Moreover, Belkin made no arrangements for his manuscripts before he died. In other words, although he had tried to publish his works before 1825, he subsequently made not the slightest attempt to safeguard them from destruction before his death in 1828. The latter circumstance can be understood as the despair and apathy of a man who had lost the desire and the will to live, a man for whom a simple cold turned out to be fatal. The sharp shift in the political climate of Russia, namely that historic catastrophe connected with the events of December 14, 1825, might well explain the change in Belkin's frame of mind and plans.

There is yet more evidence suggesting that Belkin intended to publish his tales before December, 1825. "The Snowstorm" contains a quotation from Griboedov's comedy, *Woe from Wit:* "And they tossed their caps into the air."[2] Griboedov finished work on his comedy in 1824, and Bulgarin published the first sections of it in the miscellany, *Russkaja Talija,* in January, 1825. The line quoted by Belkin, however, was not included in that edition or in the next edition which appeared in 1833[3] (after Belkin's death in any event). The quotation was taken from a monologue by Čackij that begins, "And who are the judges?" The monologue, particularly the part following the words, "A uniform! and only a uniform!" was not allowed to appear in print or to be included in the staged version. In short, this section was entirely unacceptable to the censors. Another path, however, was open to interdicted literary works: when copied by hand, such works spread among Russian readers with amazing speed.

It is well known that the Decembrists considered Griboedov's comedy excellent propaganda for the cause of freedom, and they, therefore, prepared copies of it and distributed it widely.[4] Many of their political positions were pointedly expressed in this comedy. On January 11, 1825, in exile at Mixajlovskoe, Puškin himself received a copy from I. Puščin, his lycée friend.[5]

Since Belkin could not have excerpted the quotation which appears in "The Snowstorm" from the fragment of the play that was then published, he must have quoted from one of the handwritten copies of the comedy. He could not have obtained any while he was in the army, for he retired at the very end of 1822 whereas the copies began to be prepared only in 1824. After December, 1825, the circulation of Griboedov's comedy was certainly no longer possible. Belkin evidently obtained his copy of *Woe from Wit* from one of his friends in Gorjuxino, more likely than not a former fellow officer, quite possibly the same person who later delivered Belkin's manuscript to the editor, A.P. Apparently Belkin and his mysterious friend remained in touch and exchanged literary novelties. Since Puškin himself received a copy of the comedy from one of the Decembrists, I. Puščin, it is likely that he imagined Belkin receiving his copy from someone connected with the secret organization. One may well assume that this person realized that the period following the Decembrist revolt was extremely inopportune for the publication of the tales and retained the manuscript for several years until his hand was freed by Belkin's death. With Belkin buried, the government could no longer penalize him, if through an oversight on the part of the censor the tales were published and attracted the attention of the authorities. Thus one may hypothesize that a friend of Belkin's in the Jäger regiment gave the tales to the editor, A.P., who in turn found it necessary to conceal the man's identity. The censor might have been extremely suspicious had he known of his connections. A man living in Petersburg in the winter of 1825-26 and enjoying the confidence of Belkin, the same Belkin who economically freed his serfs after being forced to retire from the 32nd Jäger regiment, might easily come under investigation in connection with the Decembrist affair. The editor, A.P., must have been well aware of the fact that the slightest connection with any participant in the Decembrist conspiracy would have resulted in a ban on the publication of the tales. These considerations are the only possible explanations for keeping secret all the information about Belkin's friend and the path the manuscript traveled to A.P.

The foreword begins with a somewhat ambiguous phrase: "Having undertaken the struggle to publish the tales of I.P. Belkin, . . ." (I, 1). The words "having undertaken" (*vzjavšis'*) may imply a request, perhaps an urgent one, by someone, while the verb, "to struggle" (*xlopotat'*), denotes the surmounting of certain obstacles. It seems that the editor, A.P., expresses himself precisely: he presumably yields to the request of Belkin's friend and undertakes the struggle with a difficult matter that he resolves owing to his experience and intelligence.

On the surface the letter represents nothing more than a testimony to the editor: "We are printing it without any changes or footnotes as a precious monument to a noble manner of thinking and a touching friendship and, at the same time, as a perfectly satisfactory biographical account." (I) A different consideration, however, may have prompted A.P. to include the letter from the neighbor in the foreword—possibly a confrontation with the government censor who would not accept anonymous manuscripts. Naturally this would have placed the editor of *The Tales of Belkin* in a difficult position. Had the government made an inquiry as to the authorship of the tales—something that it could easily have done if they seemed to reflect excessive liberalism—the editor would have found it difficult to prove that they came from the pen of the unknown and, indeed, already deceased Belkin. The censor could well have supposed "Belkin" to be a pseudonym. If A.P. deemed it unwise to reveal the name of the person who gave him the manuscript and was unable to convince the government that Belkin was indeed the author of the tales, he could not have avoided bringing suspicion upon himself for their authorship. Therefore, he proceeded to seek reliable evidence of Belkin's authorship for the sake of his own safety and not merely in order to satisfy "the justifiable curiosity of lovers of the literature of our fatherland" (I) (if he is not actually mocking the censors themselves with this phrase). From Belkin's friend who, according to this hypothesis, visited Belkin in Gorjuxino, brought him the handwritten copy of *Woe from Wit*, and possibly met Belkin's neighbor, the editor, A.P., obtained the name of the neighbor in order to request from him information on Belkin. The neighbor's letter, as it turns out, contains priceless information: the neighbor not only knew Belkin but must have had occasions to become acquainted with his tales when they were still in manuscript form, as proved irrefutably by the fact that 1) he was familiar with the toponyms in the tales (". . . the names of the hamlets and villages were borrowed from our district," (VIII)[6]) and 2) he knew that various people had told the tales to Belkin, as attested by the author's own notations in the manuscript. If an unpleasant investigation to determine the identity of the author of the tales were to be conducted, the editor could easily protect himself by quoting the written testimony of the neighbor, who was, from all indications, a conservative, loyal subject.

The role of the editor, A.P., is, therefore, considerably more significant than it first appears: he publishes the tales, codes the cycle by shifting their order, provides a key to the code, preserves the anonymity of the person who provided him with the manuscript, and places himself above suspicion of authorship of the tales through publishing the testimony of the neighbor.

The characters in the foreword are more numerous than they seem at first. The editor, A.P., is only briefly mentioned but figures prominently. Belkin's mysterious friend participates actively though invisibly. In addition, there exist two other unseen characters whose presence, nevertheless, is acutely felt: the censor, from whom the real facts of Belkin's biography must remain concealed, and the "curious researcher" to whom the same facts must be revealed by means of various clues and who is expected to enter the plot in the future and bring it to its denouement by decoding the text.

Footnotes

1. According to the neighbor, "It seems that the tales mentioned above were his first effort" (VIII). As Belkin retired by the end of 1822, he apparently wrote for six years—until his death in 1828—and produced many manuscripts, including an unfinished novel. Thus one can assume that he wrote the tales between 1823 and 1825.
2. P., v. 8, I, p. 83 (23).
3. Puškin's quotation is taken from Act 2, scene 5 of Griboedov's comedy. Bulgarin printed in *Russkaja talija* only scenes 7-10 of the first act and the entire third act. Thus the second act with Čackij's monologue was not published at that time. See: A. S. Griboedov, *Gore ot uma*, NAUKA, M., 1969, pp. 44-46 and p. 393.
4. Ibid., pp. 257-259.
5. See: *A. S. Puškin v vospominanijax sovremennikov*, M. 1974, V. I, p. 109.
6. The importance Puškin attached to this detail can be observed in his manuscript where above the word "my" in the phrase, "for which reason my own village is mentioned somewhere" (VIII), he wrote in French in different ink *"voilà."* See: P., v. 8, II, p. 590, footnote 1.

CHAPTER 3

THE CORRESPONDENCE BETWEEN THE EDITOR AND THE NEIGHBOR

Puškin's *The Tales of the Late Ivan Petrovič Belkin* is the collaboration of two fictitious authors: Belkin and the editor, A.P., whose foreword, "From the Editor," comprises a six tale epistolary in form.[1] Although only one letter—that of Belkin's neighbor—is actually presented, the contents of the editor's letter to him may be inferred from the neighbor's summary. Thus a correspondence is the main device for advancing the plot. The epistolary form minimizes the presence of the narrator and creates the impression of reliable documentation of the information requested about Belkin. This impression, however, begins to fade as soon as the text undergoes a closer examination which questions the editor's candor in his correspondence with the neighbor and introduction to the neighbor's reply. The editor pretends to know nothing of Belkin. In fact, however, it is almost certain that the editor was familiar with the more important details of Belkin's life, since A.P. was in touch with someone who knew Belkin well and who must have given the editor the name and address of Belkin's neighbor.

There is much more to the exchange between editor and neighbor than meets the eye. The neighbor receives a request for Belkin's biography from a man who apparently knows nothing of Belkin. With this assumption the neighbor composes a reply focusing only on Belkin's lack of managerial ability while concealing important details of his life which would tarnish the honor of the family name if they became public. The editor's comments on the neighbor's letter suggest, however, that A.P. understands the reason for the neighbor's omissions and misrepresentations in Belkin's biography. Thus the text is, in Baxtin's term,[2] vari-directional with a hidden, internal polemic, and with several real and feigned points of view.

The vari-directionality of the text is apparent in the semantic surplus, or overload, of certain lexemes and phrases in both the editor's and the neighbor's language. One example is the first phrase of the foreword, "*Vzjavšis' xlopotat'*," meaning "having begun to work on . . ." (I, 1). *Vzjavšis'* further connotes a commitment to undertake some mission, perhaps at another's request, and *xlopotat'*, besides simple work or action,

41

suggests an effort to surmount certain obstacles. Thus the opening words of the editor's text contain a bi-directional utterance aimed partly at the general reader, partly at the "curious researchers."

The editor actually addresses himself to four different audiences. In the first sentence of the foreword the noun, *"publika"* in *"predlagaemyx nyne publike"* ("herewith presented to the public"), is used to indicate the general Russian reader. The same noun with the same meaning is repeated in the conclusion of the foreword: ". . . *nadeemsja, čto publika ocenit ix iskrennost' i dobrodušie"* ("we trust that our public will appreciate its sincerity and goodness"). In the first footnote to the neighbor's letter, however, the editor refers to a reader with some degree of critical acumen and labels him *čitatel'*: ". . . *vpročem, uverjaem čitatelja, čto on ničego predosuditel'nogo pamjati Ivana Petroviča Belkina v sebe ne zaključaet"* ("however, we assure the reader that it contains nothing prejudicial to the memory of Ivan Petrovič Belkin"). The editor's second footnote is addressed to the next rank of readers who possess considerably greater analytical ability: *"Vypisyvaem dlja ljubopytnyx izyskatelej . . ."* ("We extract [them] for the curious researchers"). This third type of reader is actually an investigator, or researcher, and his task in establishing the real intent of the foreword and Belkin's tales is most important. He is not, however, the only one who displays considerable curiosity about Belkin's life and philosophy. The first sentence of the editor's text refers to an enigmatic category of readers: ". . . *my želali k onym prisovokupit' xotja kratkoe žizneoposanie pokojnogo avtora i tem otčasti udovletvorit' spravedlivomu ljubopytstvu ljubitelej otečestvennoj slovesnosti."* ("we wished to preface them with a brief account of the life of the late author and thereby to satisfy in part the justifiable curiosity of lovers of the literature of our fatherland.") (Text A). The *"ljubiteli otečestvennoj slovesnosti"* ("lovers of the literature of our fatherland") are linked by virtue of their curiosity with the *"ljubopytnye izyskateli"* (*ljubopytstvo* and *ljubopytnye*) ("curious researchers"—curiosity and curious). As particular information is offered to each, evidently both are assumed to be investigators. The vari-directionality of the foreword is thus established in the very first sentence which contains references to both *"publika"* (public) and *"ljubiteli otečestvennoj slovesnosti"* ("lovers of the literature of our fatherland"). The foreword is addressed on the surface to the general public (*publika*) and obliquely to two groups of analytical readers—the *ljubiteli* (lovers) and the *izyskateli* (researchers).

These two categories of analytical readers differ, however, in their disposition towards the text. While the *ljubopytnye* (*curious*) *izyskateli* (researchers) are inconspicuously introduced only in the editor's second footnote, the *ljubiteli* (lovers) in the very first sentence of the foreword attract one's attention because of the verbose style containing consonance, semantic overtones, and rhythm, a set of stresses on the third syllables of the first two words and on the second syllables of the following three words in the phrase *"spravedlívomu ljubopýtstvu ljubítelej otéčestvennoj slovésnosti"* ("the justifiable curiosity of lovers of the literature of our fatherland"), where the accent falls only on the sounds, *i*, *y*, and *e*, all of which are other than low vowels. Furthermore, there are either four or five syllables in each word forming the pattern: 5, 4, 4, 5, 4. The entire phrase is saturated with the sound *l*, which occurs five times (twice repeated in the morpheme, *ljub-*), and the consonantal clusters, *spr-*, *-tstv-*, *-stv-*, *-st-*, *-dl-*, and *sl-*. This sound and stress arrangement lends a formal, bureaucratic tone to the phrase, *"ljubitelej otečestvennoj slovesnosti"* ("lovers of the literature of our fatherland"). The curiosity of these lovers of native literature is modified by the epithet, *spravedlivyj* (justifiable), which jars in this context. Puškin used the adjective, *spravedlivyj* (justifiable), to mean either objective and fair or true and correct.[3] In the neighbor's letter, for example, this adjective is used in its second meaning to refer to Belkin's tales: *"Oni, kak skazyval Ivan Petrovič, bol'šeju častiju spravedlivy i slyšany im ot raznyx osob"* ("As Ivan Petrovič said, they are for the most part, true stories which he had heard from various people"). In the editor's phrase, however, the expected meaning would be a justifiable, or natural, curiosity, an attribute which Puškin usually expressed with the adjective, *ponjatnyj* (understandable) or *estestvennyj* (natural).[4] The epithet, *spravedlivyj* (justifiable), in this context, however, reverberates with semantic overtones of justice carrying with it all the related ideas of judicial procedures and, by extension, the government. Thus *spravedlivyj* (justifiable) reinforces the bureaucratic flavor of the set phrase, *"ljubitelej otečestvennoj slovesnosti"* ("lovers of the literature of our fatherland"), and gives the impression of interest in native literature on the part of some governmental institution. The only connection between the government and literature was, of course, the censor whom the editor sought to circumvent by establishing Belkin's authorship.

The editor's surplus of epithets adds to the vari-directionality of the text. *"My posledovali semu sovetu, i na pis'mo naše polučili niželedujuščij želaemyj otvet"* ("We followed this advice and received the following satisfactory [desirable] reply to our letter") is the next instance with a vari-directional utterance indicated by the epithet, *želaemyj* (desirable). The participle of the verb, *želat'* (to desire), may refer to an object that is desired (this is how the general reader, *publika* (public), perceives it in this context), or it can refer to the quality of a desired object. From the context it appears to the more analytical reader, *izys-*

katel' (researcher), that the first meaning would imply a redundancy, since the editor has already described at some length his extensive search for a biography of Belkin. The second meaning, which, therefore, must prevail, indicates that the editor has specific expectations and stipulations as to the information requested of the neighbor. A.P.'s requirements, which have already been described in this chapter, were met, and thus irrefutable proof of Belkin's authorship was established.

The last sentence of the editor's introduction to the neighbor's letter contains three vari-directional utterances: *"Pomeščaem ego bezo vsjakix peremen i primečanij, kak dragocennyj pamjatnik blagorodnogo obraza mnenij i trogatel'nogo družestva, a vmeste s tem, kak i ves'ma dostatočnoe biografičeskoe izvestie"* ("We are printing it without any changes or footnotes as a precious monument to a noble manner of thinking and a touching friendship and, at the same time, as a perfectly satisfactory biographical account") (Text B). The promise to refrain from making any changes or adding any footnotes has already been analyzed in the first chapter. While assuring the general reader (*publika*) that the neighbor's letter will be treated with the utmost respect, it draws the attention of the researcher (*izyskatel'*) to the second footnote. The phrase, *"kakdragocennyj pamjatnik blagorodnogo obraza mnenij"* ("as a precious monument to a noble manner of thinking"), considered a cliché by the general reader, actually refers to the neighbor's noble philosophy which cannot be explained except as his attempts to protect the honor of Belkin's father's name by misrepresenting the deeds of his son. This phrase, as well as the following one, *"ves'ma dostatočnoe biografičeskoe izvestie"* ("a perfectly satisfactory biographical account") accepted by the public at face value, recalls for the researcher the message of the epithet, *želaemyj* (desirable). Despite the fact that Belkin's biography is completely unsatisfactory, Belkin's authorship has been established to the editor's satisfaction.

Most significant, however, is the fact that text B is construed much as text A, which has been analyzed previously in terms of lexicon and consonance. The sentence concluding the editor's introduction to the neighbor's letter (text B) is considerably longer than text A (twentynine words versus seven) and consists of three sound units which contain internal consonance as well as consonantal relationships with the others. The first unit consists of seven words and sounds approximately: [pəmiščájim jivó bizʌ vs'ákix pirimén i primičánij].[5] The only verb and the two nouns which this unit contains have an initial *p* sound and are further interrelated by the consonance of [pəmiščájim, primičánij], and [pirim-/ i prim-]. The second unit consisting of nine words, [kək dragʌcényj pámitnik bləgʌródnevʌ óbrəzʌ mnénij i trógətil'nəvʌ družystvʌ], continues the previous consonance of the initial *p* sound in [*pámitnik*], which also repeats the vowel sequence of [*pəmiščá-/primičá-*]. The sound system of the second unit is formed by the Slavonic morphemes, *drago-* and *blago-*, supported by *troga-*. The passage is saturated with the consonantal clusters of *dr-*, *br-*, and *tr-*. The third unit consists of ten words, [ʌ *vmésti s tem, kak i vis'má dʌstátəčnəe biəgrʌfíčiskəe izvéstie*], is embraced by two almost identical sound sequences, [ʌ*vmésti and izvésti*], repeating the *st* cluster (four times, supported by the twice-repeated sound *s*) which is predominant in text A.

The effect of the consonance in text B, analogous to that of the previously analyzed text A, distinguishes these two passages stylistically from the rest of the paragraph.[6] The ambiguity and irony of each of these two excerpts supplement that of the other. The first passage by virtue of its formulaic flavor refers to an investigator in some governmental institution, perhaps a censor, while the second contains a hyperbolically laudable reference to the neighbor's letter. If anyone was meant to peruse the neighbor's letter, it was certainly the censor, for it was precisely for him that the editor, A.P., undertook the search for Belkin's biography. These two stylistically linked passages thus can be made to form a syntactic unit:

> [*Daby*] *otčasti udovletvorit' spravedlivomu ljubopytstvu ljubitelej otečestvennoj slovesnosti* . . . [text A], *pomeščaem ego bezo vsjakix peremen i primečanij, kak dragocennyj pamjatnik blagorodnogo obraza mnenij i trogatel'nogo družestva, a vmeste s tem, kak i ves'ma dostatočnoe biografičeskoe izvestie* [text B] (to satisfy in part the justifiable curiosity of lovers of the literature of our fatherland [text A], we are printing it without any changes or footnotes as a precious monument to a noble manner of thinking and a touching friendship and, at the same time, as a perfectly satisfactory biographical account [text B].

This sentence composed of two passages (text A and text B) stylistically distinguished from the rest of the paragraph expresses the editor's real intention, namely to establish a defense for himself in case a confrontation with the censor should become unavoidable. Thus the editor is addressing the general public (*publika*), as well as the thoughtful reader (*čitatel'*), and the censor ("*ljubiteli otečestvennoj slovesnosti*"), ("lovers of the literature of our fatherland"), as well as the curious researcher ("*ljubopytnyj izyskatel'* "). The editor publishes Belkin's biography in code for the censor while helping the researcher decode it.

The neighbor's letter also contains bi-directional utterances although they are addressed to parties other than those for whom the editor intended his message. The neighbor's reader is only one—the editor, A.P., who presumably knows nothing of Belkin. In the neighbor's tone, nevertheless, one can detect a tense, internal dialogue between him and an imaginary critical guardian who seeks to prevent any damaging information from slipping into Belkin's biography and, on the other hand, a dialogue between the neighbor and his conscience which feels uncomfortable with the lies demanded by the guardian. Several inconsistencies, and slips of the pen in the neighbor's letter reveal his state of mind. His references to the honor of the Belkin family (III) are completely superfluous, for the Belkins were noblemen, a class whose honor and respectability were not normally subject to question. Furthermore, the fact that Belkin is honorable and meek (VI) can easily be inferred by the reader from the other details. However, the neighbor's description of Belkin indicates the former's quarrel with himself in that he emphasizes exactly those qualities that would contrast with a conservative's conception of revolutionaries as dishonorable, treacherous, and criminal. A meek man of honor is quite the opposite of the traditional portrait of a revolutionary conspirator. However, since the neighbor apparently thought the editor was unaware of Belkin's presumed connection with the Southern branch of the Decembrist conspirary, the former is defensive, not with A.P., but with the imaginary critical guardian who knows of Belkin's past and urges the neighbor to conceal it as well as possible in order to protect the honor of Belkin's family. This same guardian demands extreme brevity in the neighbor's reference to the deaths of Belkin's parents. It has already been noted that their demise could hardly have served as a convincing reason for Belkin's retirement (III, 12). In all probability both events (his retirement and the death of his parents occurring almost at the same time) were the aftermath of his involvement in a revolutionary conspiracy. The brevity of the neighbor's reference is one of the indications that he is attempting to gloss over the tragic reality of Belkin's past.

Having decided to reveal only a fragment of Belkin's life, the neighbor carefully invents an excuse for all his omissions. In both the opening and concluding paragraphs of his letter he emphasizes that the biography contains only the information that he can recall (II, XI). As the letter is written only two years after Belkin's death, the neighbor's memory of his friend should be fresh and his excuses unnecessary. Nevertheless, they are quite consistent with his strategy, for on the pretext of forgetting he omits the number of Belkin's Jäger regiment (III, 10). As such an excuse would have been superfluous if it had been meant for the editor who was presumably unaware of Belkin's past, the neighbor is thus silencing his guilty conscience which is due to the lies and misrepresentations he feels obliged to include in Belkin's biography. The best example of the neighbor's defensiveness is his assurance that Belkin's introduction of the toponym, Nenaradovo, in one of his tales is not due to some mischief or ill intention (VIII). The suspicion would never have entered anyone's mind if the neighbor himself had not suggested it. Here his internal dialogue becomes apparent, now not arising from the need to preserve strict confidentiality in regard to many facts in Belkin's biography, but rather from the neighbor's desire to hide his wounded pride. The reason for his sensitiveness remains unknown; it merely serves to establish some link between Belkin's biography and the tale, "The Snowstorm," in which the toponym, Nenaradovo, occurs.

In the neighbor's letter the most revealing symptoms of his schizoid point of view are several slips of the pen. At the beginning he states that he is writing with "great pleasure" (II); at the end, however, he asks the editor not to reveal his name to the public on the pretext of the impropriety of a man of his age joining the ranks of the literati, or those who invent stories, i.e. *sočiniteli* (XI), as if a truthful account of one's friend's life would make anyone a *sočinitel'*. In reality, however, the neighbor is not inconsistent as may at first appear. As his version of Belkin's biography is less than the whole truth, he is embarrassed for his lies and omissions and inadvertently reveals his discomfort by voicing his fear of being accused of becoming a *sočinitel'*.

To the neighbor's lapses about his friendship with Belkin must be added his highly controversial statement: "This matter did not disturb our friendly relations in any way, however . . . although in habits, manner of thinking, and disposition we had very little in common for the most part" (VI, 18). The neighbor's feelings toward Belkin constantly veer from one extreme to the other, from paternal pity and affection to open condemnation and alienation culminating in this admission. The contradiction in this paragraph clearly shows that the neighbor imposed his friendship on Belkin, that this role was an uncomfortable one, and that in his letter which provides him occasion to define his relationship with Belkin he is releasing repressed feelings when he enumerates their differences. Apparently these two "friends" were completely alien to each other. This slip of the pen may lead the reader to question why the neighbor forced himself on Belkin. The answer to this as well as to several other questions may be found in the neighbor's phrase: "As a friend of Ivan Petrovič's late parent, I considered it my duty to offer my advice to the son too" (V). The key word here is "duty." The neighbor's last *lapsus calami* is evident in his incorrect dating of his letter revealing that the number, sixteen, which happens to be the number of Belkin's infantry division, was on the writer's mind (II, 5; III, 10; XII, 31).

The composition of the neighbor's letter itself demonstrates his reluctance to reveal Belkin's full biography. The direct references to Belkin comprise only fifty-six percent of the volume of the letter;[7] the rest are distributed among the neighbor himself (twenty-eight percent), Belkin's housekeeper (six percent), Belkin's father (four percent), the peasants (three percent), and the physician (two percent). Furthermore, Belkin's life prior to his return to Gorjuxino comprises only ten percent of the neighbor's letter. Throughout the letter the neighbor yields to a compulsion to digress from Belkin's biography into managerial details and descriptions of insignificant individuals. The digressions begin to cease after the neighbor's emotional release expressed in his enumeration of the ways in which he and Belkin differed. After having clarified their real relationship, the neighbor relaxes and begins more matter-of-factly to discuss Belkin's life style and his writings.

The disproportionately modest volume of the text devoted to Belkin yields a rather scanty portrait that pales even more when compared with those of the minor characters drawn with colorful, nominal epithets. These epithets contrast with those ascribed to Belkin which are without exception either dubious or redundant. Belkin is presented as a friend and neighbor of the author of the letter (II)—facts already surmised from the editor's remarks (I). Belkin is also referred to as a "young landowner" (V), a neutral designation at best, and, finally, as a "gentle and honest young man" (VI), on the surface an almost meaningless phrase as has already been noted. In contrast to these low-key descriptions of Belkin stand brief but expressive portrayals of minor characters. The reader learns that Belkin's father was a second major and, though not wealthy, "moderate and extremely shrewd in business matters" (III). The church reader was a "revered man," to whom Belkin owed "his love of reading and studying Russian literature" (III). Belkin's housekeeper was a "stupid old woman" who could not distinguish one banknote from another and who was a godmother to all the peasants' children (VI). The village elder is always referred to as a swindler (V), and the local doctor was "a man of great skill, particularly in the treatment of chronic diseases, such as corns and the like" (IX). The contrast between this colorful, expressive background and the pallid image of Belkin projected on it clearly indicates the neighbor's multiple points of view and perhaps even his subconscious reluctance to apply his literary talents to Belkin in order to define his personality as well.

Footnotes

1. The first critic to consider the editor's foreword as a sixth tale was Jan M. Meijer: " 'The Sixth Tale of Belkin' in *The Tales of Belkin by A. S. Puškin*," The Hague, Mouton, 1968, pp. 110-134, especially pp. 113-117. An outline of my chapter with the observation that the editor's foreword contains a plot was presented in my article, "Šifr Puškina," in *Novyj žurnal*, New York, 1970, pp. 80-94. The concept of the foreword as a sixth tale is further supported in a recent study by S. G. Bočarov: *Poetika Puškina*, op. cit., pp. 140, 147. See also the Introduction to this book.
2. See: M. Baxtin: *Problemy poetiki Dostoevskogo*, M., 1963, especially pp. 242-273. In English translation see: *Readings in Russian Poetics: Formalist and Structuralist Views*, edited by Ladislav Matejka and Krystyna Pomorska, M.I.T. Press, Cambridge, Mass., 1971, pp. 176-196.
3. See: *Slovar' jazyka Puškina*, M., 1956.
4. Ibid.
5. This phonetic transcription, as well as the following ones, includes only those phonetic features that are essential for this study.
6. V. Vinogradov established the bureaucratic flavor of the editor's discourse in the foreword. However, one must distinguish the degree to which different parts of this text reflect a bureaucratic style. Between texts A and B such expressions as *obratitis' bylo my . . . no, k sožaleniju . . . ona sovetovala nam* interject a less formal tone. See: V. V. Vinogradov, op. cit., pp. 539-540.
7. This percentage would be even lower if the long passage describing the neighbor's interrogation of the village elder were not counted as dealing with Belkin.

CHAPTER 4

PUŠKIN'S CODE

It still remains to be examined whether Puškin did not simply choose at random all the details in the foreword. His first draft of the neighbor's letter begins with the sentence: "I am sincerely happy that the manuscript that I had the honor to forward to you appeared worthy of your attention. I am hurrying to fulfill your wish by furnishing you with all the information I was able to obtain concerning my deceased friend."[1] The difference between this and the final draft is that in the first the neighbor fulfills two functions: he provides the editor not only with Belkin's biography but actually with the manuscript itself. In other words, in this first draft the means by which Belkin's manuscript reaches the editor is clear. One might expect that the earlier draft would have been less lucid than the later one and that in rewriting, Puškin might have attempted to elucidate facts, explain related circumstances, and rectify outright inconsistencies. In fact, as he rewrote, he employed the reverse strategy purposely introducing vagueness, ambiguity, and contradiction. In the final version the process by which the manuscript found its way to the editor, A.P., is completely separated from the information provided about Belkin. While the path the manuscript took is coded with much greater care, pertinent details of Belkin's military career are purposely omitted.[2] Even after Puškin had written the first draft of the foreword, he presumably was still uncertain how to present the various ruses and strategies that A.P. would use to bypass the censors. The second and final draft begins with the following sentence that Puškin subsequently crossed out: "The manuscript, the collection of the tales now offered to the public for judgment, was delivered to us by M.I.B., a close relative and heiress of the author."[3] It is no longer the neighbor but a certain female relative referred to by her initials who delivered the manuscript to the editor. But Puškin rejected this ruse as well and proceeded to write the published version in which Belkin's manuscript reaches the editor, A.P., in a mysterious way.

This progression was not haphazard or coincidental. The history of the writing of this very important part of the cycle reveals Puškin's conscious search for a method of introducing an additional character without mentioning him—that intermediary who, in addition to fulfilling other functions, gave Belkin's manuscript to A.P. Puškin solved the problem by creating a vacuum that someone had to fill. This person's character, his relationship to Belkin, and his *Weltanschauung* are indiscernible to the average reader. Here, however, Puškin was not writing for the average reader but for the "curious researchers" who would well understand his intent.

This hidden stratum imparts to the foreword a flavor distinct from that of the cycle as a whole. What is passed over in silence is more important than what is conveyed explicitly. Behind all the omissions and allusions to Belkin's mysterious friend lies a hollow, gaping expanse—the year 1825. It is not mentioned, yet all the events concealed in the introduction revolve around that fatal time.

Implication, as well as allusion, may signify reticence, but its most fundamental feature is that its meaning is impossible to prove. It states a fact without seeming to do so; it informs seemingly without revealing, commands without ordering, insults without abusing. In short, it assumes no responsibility. Puškin's use of implication partially explains why literary critics were unable to penetrate the imperturbably smooth surface of *The Tales of Belkin*. Implication and allusion can be understood only in connection with the specific information to which they refer, often in some seemingly unimportant minute details, and in most cases their meaning remains unascertainable.

Puškin, however, came to the aid of the "curious researchers," or literary students, by arranging the allusions in a well-formed system instead of presenting them as individual entities. Thus the implications become interrelated signs. The sheer multitude of concealed meanings within a system provides the basis for the decoding of the system as a whole. When each allusion without exception occupies a logical place in the entire hypothesis, then this new system ceases to be built on assumptions, and the concealed meaning within each allusion can be proved in a new context. The allusions consequently change their nature; they are no longer ambiguous but are transformed into clear, definite signs. It is this kind of system, or code, that Puškin creates in *The Tales of Belkin*.

The ambiguity of a given implication can be illustrated by the titles of the tales as they appear in the editor's footnote. The changed arrangement by itself is insignificant. Only when it is considered in conjunction with the opening of "The Stationmaster" (see the next chapter) and with the signs concerning the unusual circumstances of Belkin's retirement does it become meaningful as part of a complex system.

Puškin provides the literary student with all the information necessary for an analysis of his tales. In addition to building a system of concealed meanings, he arranges the allusions on various levels of perceptibility, thus granting the "researchers" access to the actual essence of his work. Certain implications lie on the very surface of the narrative and serve as obvious signals (the dates of the letters (II, 5; XII, 31) and the promise not kept by the editor (I, 4; VII, 19; VIII, 24)). They provide clues to the other contradictions in the text of which there are far too many to ascribe merely to the oversights of the author. Examining further, one finds information of great import (the order of the tales in Belkin's manuscript (VIII, 26)) and the economic liberation of the Gorjuxino serfs (IV, 15). Finally, one notices the allusions to Belkin's political life—his fate in the 32nd Jäger infantry regiment (III, 10), the mysterious circumstances of his retirement (III, 12), his friend (who holds similar views and serves as an intermediary (I, 3)), the Lancaster System of instruction, and the manuscript copy of *Woe from Wit*—in short, to the Kišinev group of Decembrists.

Doubtless critics would have decoded the foreword easily had they not been hypnotized for many years by the apparent irony of the entire text on which they frequently commented. For example, they felt that the editor's attitude toward the neighbor was ironic, for it praises him for his friendship and "noble manner of thinking," while his philistinism and provincialism are all too obvious. It turns out, however, that the irony in the foreword is only a façade. After a more thorough examination one must conclude that the editor's laudable references to Belkin's neighbor and his letter must be taken at face value.

The foreword, "From the Editor," can no longer be considered merely an introduction; it is constructed around a hidden, complex, and absorbing plot. Therefore, it should be considered a separate tale central to the cycle. It reveals the real Belkin and discloses the ruses of the editor, A.P., his multi-layered code, and his devices for fooling the censor.

Footnotes

1. P., v. 8, II, p. 581.
2. In the course of his work Puškin made another change in the foreword. In the original draft he implied much more overtly that Belkin freed his serfs and at the same time was less specific as to the neighbor's views on serfdom. In the first draft the neighbor describes Belkin's negligence as a landowner:
    I advised him at least to institute a quit-rent system for the peasants and thereby to spare himself any concern over management. My proposal met with his approval, yet he did not implement it for lack of time.—Meanwhile, production declined; the peasants did not pay the quit-rent and stopped fulfilling the corvée, so that in the entire district there was no landowner who was more loved and who received less income.

The first draft of the foreword ends here. The last sentence is particularly important; in it Puškin states directly what the reader of the final version is left to surmise—namely, that the peasants did not work under the corvée system, nor did they pay quit-rent. Hence, Belkin's income was reduced to zero. In the second draft of the foreword, Puškin obscures this point though he preserves the essential ideas and images. Thus Belkin's excuse of lack of time to establish quit-rent for the peasants is replaced by his feigned nap during the neighbor's interrogation of the village elder. The second draft is more complex, contains more characters, and at the same time depends heavily on allusion.
See: P., v. 8, II, p. 583.
3. Ibid.

PART II

SECOND READING

Chapter 1

BELKIN'S VARIANT

The editor, A.P., in his second footnote lists the tales in a different order from the one published. The published sequence, which will be referred to as Variant I, is "The Shot," "The Snowstorm," "The Undertaker," "The Stationmaster," "Mistress into Maid." The tales ordered according to Belkin's manuscript as listed in A.P.'s footnote will be called Variant II: "The Stationmaster," "The Shot," "The Undertaker," "The Snowstorm," and "Mistress into Maid."

In Belkin's manuscript the collection of tales opened with "The Stationmaster" while the published version opens with "The Shot." "The Stationmaster" stands out among the tales because of its long and stylistically unique introduction. In Belkin's sequence (Variant II) this introduction to "The Stationmaster" with the narrator, A.G.N.'s personal reflections and reminiscences appears at the very beginning of the cycle. The first character to appear in Variant II is neither the stationmaster, Samson Vyron, nor his daughter, Dunja, but the Titular Counsellor, A.G.N. Therefore, the "curious researcher" must take a closer look at this character and try to determine his personality and philosophy, as well as his relation to Puškin's ideas and past experiences.

The introduction to "The Stationmaster" spans three stylistically distinct paragraphs. The verbosity and emotionalism of the first paragraph colored with rhetorical questions, exclamations, and hyperbole is somehow alien to Puškin's style:

> Who has not cursed stationmasters, who has not quarrelled with them? Who, in a moment of anger, has not demanded from them the fatal book in order to enter into it an unavailing complaint of unjust treatment, rudeness and carelessness? Who does not consider them outcasts of mankind, equivalent to the bribe-hungry clerks of the past or at least to the robbers of Murom?[1]

A.G.N., however, went on to abandon the verbosity of the first paragraph and proceeded with his introduction in less colorful and somewhat more restrained manner:

> It can easily be guessed that I have friends among the venerable stationmasters. Indeed, the memory of one of them is particularly dear to me. Circumstances once brought us together, and it is of him that I now intend to speak to my indulgent readers.[2]

Stylistically this section of the introduction to the story is representative of the entire cycle. The narration here is lucid and rapid as is typical of Puškin. The paragraph that follows, however, bears the stamp of yet another style in his prose and deserves close analysis. This third and final paragraph is somewhat misleading. The first sentence marks the beginning of the narration proper, and one is made to feel that the introduction is over:

> In the month of May, 1816, I happened to be travelling through the province of *** on a road now no longer in existence.[3]

The specificity here, in fact, sharply distinguishes the passage from the somewhat general comments on stationmasters in the first paragraph. Yet the impression that the introduction has ended proves to be false, for in the following two sentences Puškin's narrator reverts to his personal reminiscences which have little to do with the tale itself:

> I was low in rank, I travelled by post and could only pay for two horses. As a result, stationmasters treated me unceremoniously, and I often had to take by force that which was mine by right.[4]

This passage recalls both the first part of the introduction with its sharp criticism of stationmasters and the epigraph to the tale:

> The collegiate registrar
> is the dictator of the post-station.[5]

The arbitrariness and dictatorial manner of stationmasters are sensed even more strongly in the fourth sentence:

> Being young and hot-headed, I was indignant at the baseness and cowardice of the stationmaster when he harnessed the horses which had already been prepared for my troika to the carriage of a senior official.[6]

At this point A.G.N. temporarily interrupts his discussion of stationmasters to focus on the more general themes of despotism and arbitrariness. His language becomes harsher, more terse, and he switches his attention to a higher social milieu. Obviously then the despotism and arbitrariness he criticizes are not confined to the lower ranks of society:

> . . . I could not get used to being passed over by some discriminating serf at the Governor's table.[7]

The analogy becomes clear here. Just as the "collegiate registrar" (the official title of a stationmaster) is a dictator, so is the governor of the province, and A.G.N. finds himself passed over willfully by both. The hierarchy of the entire empire is thus mirrored in the post-station. Significantly the narrative tone in "The Journey to Arzrum," from which this particular episode is taken, is much more complacent. There Puškin simply exclaims: "The devil take this Tiflis Gourmet!"[8] A.G.N., however, following his gibe at the prevailing respect for rank, is quick to renounce the freedom of thought characteristic of his youth. On the subject of rank and its inherent despotism he says: "Nowadays the one and the other seem to me to be in the order of things."[9] He sees himself as looking at the world more sensibly now. Although A.G.N. has seemingly demonstrated his loyalty to the regime, he pushes his point yet further and begins to defend with tongue in cheek the system of the "table of ranks": "Indeed, what would become of us if in place of the generally accepted rule: 'let rank respect rank,' we were to apply another. . . ." A.G.N.'s penitent, conservative remarks set the tone for the passage, and one quite naturally expects a statement affirming the wisdom of this existing order. However, at the end of the sentence, ". . . for example, let intelligence respect intelligence,"[10] the entire system of values is inverted. The juxtaposition of the two concepts of intelligence and rank produces unexpected evidence for the absurdity of the existing order. However, A.G.N., witty and cautious as he is, quickly turns it all into a joke: "What arguments would arise! . . ."[11] Here, again he moves one hundred eighty degrees around the circle, and a wicked taunt slips out from behind his benign smile: "Who would resolve them?"[12] These last words were not included in the final text, for the mockery would have been too evident and most dangerous. The imperial judge, the omnipotent arbiter of all arguments, becomes the object of the Titular Counsellor's sarcasm only in Puškin's rough draft. In the final edition Puškin laughs the matter off and refers to the "Tiflis gourmet": "And whom would the servants serve dinner to first?"[13] A sharp and final transition to the actual plot of the story follows: "But to return to my tale."[14]

A simple reading of the text dealing with the rank and intelligence without careful attention to the voice of the narrator makes it difficult to detect Puškin's hidden gibe. In fact, it was mainly for the sake of the narrator's intonation that Puškin introduced *skaz*, a technique alien to his usual style. This made possible sudden and abrupt shifts, together with speech gestures and intonations, all of which were unintelligible to the censors. The third paragraph of the introduction to "The Station-master" is key, partly for its autobiographical nature and partly for the central role it plays structurally. Equally important, however, is the link it forms with the epigraph to the tale.

Throughout the introduction to the tale the image of the station-master undergoes a change. The epigraph portrays this class of civil servants as despotic: "The collegiate registrar is the dictator of the post-station." The opening paragraph of the introduction modifies this theme in that the stationmaster is viewed as misunderstood or abused by trav-ellers. A.G.N. characterizes stationmasters as highly honorable and good-natured—in any event, far from despotic. Gradually then A.G.N. cas-ually begins to prepare his readers for a reappraisal of the commonly accepted notion of respect for rank: "As for me, I confess that I prefer their [stationmasters'] conversation to that of some sixth-class official travelling on government business."[15] Implicit in this remark is the fact that A.G.N., an intelligent man himself, judges those with whom he talks by their native intelligence. The metamorphosis of the stationmaster thus proceeds in stages. Initially he is portrayed as a dictator, then as a peace-ful, good man, and finally as an interesting companion. By the beginning of the third paragraph of the introduction, he has already bcome a friend of the narrator. Finally, in the fourth paragraph, A.G.N. views post-masters with the eyes of youth, and they are, seemingly, transformed once more into petty dictators. It must be kept in mind, however, that Puškin, at this point in the introduction, is no longer concerned with stationmasters as such; they serve merely as a pretext for his discussion of the antithesis between intelligence and rank, and in that light their despotism acquires imperial dimensions embodying the pervasive canon of the "table of ranks." It is precisely to this paragraph that the epigraph to the entire tale pointedly refers. The stationmaster is transformed from the dictator of one post-station into an emblem of the dictatorship of the state, thereby assuming the characteristics described in the epigraph. The epigraph bears no relation to the tale itself; it would be difficult to call Samson Vyrin a dictator even in jest. The fact that the epigraph relates not to the story but merely to the fourth paragraph of the introduction speaks well for the importance that Puškin attached to the passage in question and the narrator, Titular Counsellor A.G.N.

Thematically this passage touches upon several aspects of Puškin's life. The opposition of intelligence or genius to rank and power colored the age in which Puškin lived. The imperial judge of Puškin's art at that time was Nicholas I. Such a situation could exist only if rank respected rank, for who would arbitrate between the poet and the emperor if the foundation of the world were "let intelligence respect intelligence"? Furthermore, for four years Puškin had been involved in an argument with the emperor (if one can, in fact, speak of arguments in such a case). Puškin stated in his note "On Popular Education," which he wrote for Nicolas I in November, 1826:

> Ranks have become the passion of the Russian people. Peter the Great wanted it, and the condition of Russia at that time demanded it. In other countries a young man completes his course of study in about twenty-five years; here he rushes to enter the service as soon as possible, for he must be a colonel or a collegiate councillor by the age of thirty. He goes out into the world without any basic knowledge, . . .[16]

Several lines later Puškin turned his attention to practical measures:

> Of course, the abolition of ranks (at least of civil ranks) offers great advantages: but, like any general changes in decrees which are sanctified by time and habit, this measure also carries with it limitless confusion. It is possible, at least, to derive a certain benefit from this abuse and to present ranks as the object and prerogative of education; . . .[17]

Puškin's point is well taken. Even if one is forced to accept the system of ranks as an intrinsic part of society, it is necessary, nevertheless, to abolish a system forcing young people to sacrifice their education for the sake of rank, and in the future rank should be awarded on the basis of intelligence and education.

Puškin conveyed these thoughts through the character of A.G.N. and proposed a system in which the two maxims—"let rank respect rank" and "let intelligence respect intelligence"—would no longer contradict but would complement each other. The excerpt below from the manuscript of "The Stationmaster" argues well for the fact that Puškin had precisely these remarks in "On Popular Education" in mind while he was writing the introduction to the story: "Now the one and the other seem to me to be in the order of things, and the golden rule, 'let rank respect rank,' does not appear to be the destruction of mankind."[18] Puškin had obviously tempered his judgment with caution.

Benkendorf's letter to Puškin attests to the Emperor's cool reception of "On Popular Education":

> His Majesty deigned to observe, concerning your note, that the rule which you have accepted, that of education and genius serving as the sole basis for perfection, is dangerous to the general tranquility

and has lured you, yourself, to the edge of the abyss into which
have plunged such a great number of young people. One should
prefer morals, diligent service and zeal to inexperienced, immoral,
and purposeless education.[19]

Thus the system as it stood was based on the opposition of "education
and genius" to "morals, diligent service, and zeal." Though Puškin did
not use the word "genius" in his note, Count Benkendorf responded for
Nicholas I very harshly, emphasizing what he felt to be a dichotomy:
"genius" on the one hand and "diligent service" on the other. Puškin's
reply came four years later through A.G.N. Although, as noted above,
it was softened in the published text, the sarcasm, nonetheless, retained its
sting.

    A.G.N.'s bold, caustic remarks undoubtedly were intended to serve
as more than merely the prologue to one tale. Appearing at the beginning of the cycle, they would have tended not only to color the tone of
"The Stationmaster" but to reverberate throughout the subsequent tales
as well. However, as "The Stationmaster" is the next-to-last story in the
cycle as it is published, the sarcastic tone of A.G.N.'s opening is muted
by the preceding tales which, in turn, appear to lack a unifying theme.

    The placement of "The Stationmaster" in the cycle colors the
reader's perception of the humor and irony in the tale. "Mistress into
Maid" is a cheerful and patently happy tale regardless of its placement.
As for the others, there is a certain amount of irony and humor (even
if it is black humor)—in "The Shot" in the scene in the Count's study
and in "The Snowstorm" during Burmin's wild escapade in the blizzard
and in the ironic description of the two lovers. "The Undertaker" needs
no commentary in this respect. In Variant I (i.e., the order in which the
tales actually appear in print) the caustic prologue to "The Stationmaster"
directly following the ludicrous, tale, "The Undertaker," also appears
humorous. In any event, in light of the three preceding stories the introduction to "The Stationmaster" naturally tends to be interpreted in a
humorous rather than a sarcastic vein. The replacement of respect for
rank with another maxim, respect for intelligence, is reduced to a wit-
ticism, particularly after A.G.N. exclaims: "What arguments would arise!
And whom would the servants serve dinner to first?"[20] The same may
apply to another of A.G.N.'s remarks: "As for me, I confess that I prefer
their [fourteenth-class officials'] conversation to that of some six-class
official travelling on government business."[21] The sting in these remarks
would register more strongly on the reader were "The Stationmaster"
not preceded by the three tales as they appear in Variant I.

    In all the three tales preceding "The Stationmaster" the denouement is sudden and contradicts what might naturally be expected to happen. To the reader who is prepared for a continuation of this technique the prologue to "The Stationmaster," likewise, seems surprising and amusing. But with the transition from the first to the second variant the mood of the cycle changes. It is colored now, not by Silvio's duel in "The Shot" (Variant I), but by A.G.N.'s opening remarks in "The Stationmaster" (Variant II) which are perceived afresh without an anticipatory smile.

In light of Belkin's biography and his political and intellectual bent, one common characteristic of his five tales becomes most significant. Each tale has a happy ending but, at the same time, behind this joyful development of the plot there exists a sad circumstance.

In each tale there is a satisfying denouement of the central conflict. Dunja marries and leads a happy life; Silvio spares the Count and grows morally in his role as a defender of freedom; the undertaker brushes away the horrors of his nightmare; Marja Gavrilovna attracts the proposal of her lawful husband; and, finally, Alexej marries Liza-Akulina, who turns out to be his social equal.

But if the analysis is discontinued at this point, an essential element in the tales remains unexplored; namely, that the mood of the tales, with the exception of "Mistress into Maid," is always dualistic. Beneath what appears to be a reassuring, elated note lies another motif that stops significantly short of optimism. Samson Vyrin's death from despair in "The Stationmaster" and Vladimir's self-destruction in "The Snowstorm" are cases in point. Less obvious, but equally important, is the Count's shame at his dishonorable shot at Silvio, and the undertaker's realization that he is the only craftsman who never will be able to raise a friendly toast to his clients.

This dual mood allows I. P. Belkin to introduce the two contrasting philosophies of internal freedom and self-enslavement through two diametrically opposed types of characters. One type is resourceful, broadminded, and independent; the other is ruled by societal, cultural, and religious conventions and is, consequently, prevented from thinking, reacting, or living authentically. The despotic and artificial convictions that inevitably lead the latter character type to his total or, at least, partial destruction in the first four tales is contrasted to the adventurous and carefree *Weltanschauung* of the internally free characters who play major roles in the exultant conclusions in all five tales.

Furthermore, those characters who were endowed by Belkin with inner independence violate, in one way or another, customary patterns of behavior and, at certain points, commonly accepted ethical standards. Dunja's elopement with Minskij, Burmin's bizarre prank at the Žadrino church are the clearest examples. But even Jurko's tactless, albeit humorous, suggestion to Adrijan favorably contrasts with Adrijan's false professional pride.

In each story symbols of social ethics or cultural pressures on the individual are manifested. In "The Stationmaster" the illustrations of the parable of the prodigal son on the walls of Vyrin's house indicate the father's frame of reference and the mechanics of his destruction; in "The Shot" the veneration of the code of honor and bravery, as well as the unconditional acceptance of the institution of the duel, is emphasized in the first chapter of the tale through the young narrator, I.L.P.; and one can see the artificial origin of the romantic love between Marja Gavrilovna and Vladimir in "The Snowstorm."

The general scheme of the first four tales written by Belkin is rather obvious. At the beginning of each story one or two characters, totally conditioned by social or cultural factors, appear. In the course of the tale Belkin introduces an intrinsically independent character who commits an unconventional act and emerges unscathed. This scheme is slightly complicated by the presentation of some characters as static and some as undergoing spiritual and intellectual development. There are really two Dunjas: the first, the young, attractive girl, and the second, a married woman who weeps at the grave of her father. There are two Silvios: the first, the one who leaves the small town to continue his duel with the Count; the second, the one who brings his feud to an end without bloodshed and who later sacrifices his own life in a struggle for the independence of other people. There are also two Burmins: the totally carefree hussar officer who, for no reason, marries an unknown girl and the Burmin who falls desperately in love with Marja Gavrilovna. However, no matter how the individual characters change their roles and places in these tales, the overall pattern is carried out in Belkin's first four stories with remarkable consistency. At the end of each story the reader is faced with an independent, inwardly free character while the opponents or antagonists vanish or remain psychologically maimed before the outcome of the story. This second layer of the plot contributes some sadness to the otherwise happy endings of the four tales.

"Mistress into Maid," as the concluding tale in the cycle, presents a very different picture. The sequence of coincidences, caprices, and pranks is not organized along two parallel lines as in the preceding four tales. No one is victimized; no one perishes. All the characters are free; they live joyously and naturally. With the exception of Miss Jackson, a comic old spinster who stands out because of her own limitations, no one takes traditions or customs seriously. However, even in this, the most vivacious tale in the cycle, the opening is overshadowed by conventional prejudices and inflexibility. The neighbors are feuding inexplicably but bitterly. Alexej wears the aura of a disillusioned romantic, although he is ready to discard this role at the first opportunity. Liza cannot formally meet Alexej because of the ill-feeling between their parents, and it is difficult to foresee how she will find a way out of this predicament. Quite suddenly, however, these masks, clichés, and prejudices fall away as life takes its own course and everyone begins to live authentically without concern for behavioral norms. This humorous, lighthearted tale is refreshing not only for the charm of its style and grace but for the unlimited gaiety and freedom of action inherent in virtually all of the characters.

The same dichotomy of character types is also apparent in the relationship between Belkin's two narrators, A.G.N. and I.L.P. In their relationship, however, there is no possibility of direct confrontation, since each is confined to his own text. However, the fact that there are two characters narrating two different stories in the first person and participating in the events of these tales suggests an analysis of these two narrators. It is immediately apparent that only A.G.N. is a man of original thought. Lieutenant Colonel I.L.P. lives within narrow confines, completely subordinating himself to the conventional military code of behavior.

A.G.N.'s comments on the value of rank versus intelligence indicate his liberalism. His notion of replacing respect for rank with respect for intelligence well could serve as an epigraph to the entire cycle of tales. Precisely because of the sharpness of his liberal views, A.G.N. contrasts with the narrator of "The Shot," Lieutenant Colonel I.L.P. Customary, traditional, and conventional precepts have conditioned the latter's judgment. Like many people of this ilk, he is highly intolerant. When Silvio fails to challenge the young officer R*** as the code of honor demands, I.L.P. silently rebukes Silvio and is unable to remain friendly with him even after the other officers in the regiment have dismissed the incident and have again begun to enjoy Silvio's hospitality. I.L.P.'s prejudice emerges in his reaction to both Silvio's and the Count's narrations of the two stages of the duel. When Silvio states that he endured a slap in the face six years before, I.L.P. remarks: "And you didn't fight him? Perhaps circumstances separated you?"[22] He totally discounts the possibility that Silvio might have acted in a manner not prescribed by the dueling code. When the Count relates the story of his second shot at Silvio, I.L.P. is aghast. Although taking his shot violates the dueling code, the Count's behavior is perfectly understandable; I.L.P., however, cannot grasp this.

The concluding moments of "The Shot" and "The Stationmaster" are also juxtaposed. A.G.N. is involved in the events of the plot. As he walks away from Vyrin's grave, his narration emanates warmth, for he is happy about Dunja's success in life. On the other hand, I.L.P.'s closing words in the epilogue of "The Shot" exhibit no trace of personal involvement, and the reader senses his utter indifference. The story, at best, rouses I.L.P.'s curiosity: "And thus it was that I discovered the outcome of the story whose beginning had once impressed me so deeply."[23] It is the unusual duel that intrigues him, not the fate of Silvio or the Count.

The arrangement of the tales as found in Belkin's manuscript is conducive to conveying the theme of the cycle. With the exception of "Mistress into Maid" all the tales exhibit two tones: the first, inner freedom leading to a joyous denouement; the second, inner subjugation ending in misery. In Variant II these tones occur in reverse order throughout the cycle: the first two tales are written in a minor key; the subsequent tones tend towards a major key that dominates in "Mistress into Maid." The same theme develops harmoniously on two different levels. The tales are united not only by theme as in Variant I but by their dynamic development of it so that the entire cycle can be read as an indictment of conventionality.

As the end of the cycle draws near, the gloom gradually lifts. The most pathetic death is Samson Vyrin's, in whom reader and narrator alike lose, if not a friend, then at least a very good acquaintance. Vyrin's death is tied to Dunya's good fortune. It is only through her visit to her father's grave that the reader learns of her happy fate. "The Stationmaster" is the only tale in which happiness and grief are almost inseparable.

"The Shot," which immediately follows "The Stationmaster" in Variant II, shifts markedly to a more optimistic tone, even though the threat of a tragic denouement, i.e., the murder of the Count, looms right up to the climax. Silvio's death, introduced only in the epilogue, adds a final stroke to his portrait. That there is no one to mourn his death—that he spent his life virtually alone as a reckless duelist—fails to dominate the epilogue entirely, and the image that remains is that of a regenerated man.

In "The Undertaker" death pervades life itself: Adrijan Proxorov lives side by side with death and profits from it. On the one hand, this constant association makes death seem a trivial, everyday occurrence; on the other, it places the undertaker beyond the boundaries of life and dooms him to loneliness among the people who become his clients only once—after they have died. The "death" of Trjuxina, the merchant's wife, plays, of course, only an auxiliary role. The real spectre of death appears when the watchman, Jurko, proposes that the undertaker drink to the health of his dead and when subsequently they do, in fact, arrive at Adrijan's in acceptance of his invitation. At the denouement Adrijan fortunately turns to the living. Death becomes harmless, seeming to dissolve into life, thereby once more losing its sting.

The death of Vladimir in "The Snowstorm" is even less awesome. It is ennobled coincidentally by his sacrifice for his country during a time of danger and is considerably removed from the main plot. Vladimir does not play any role in the denouement. In fact, his death, by eliminating him from the scene and emphasizing the falseness of his reactions, performs an auxiliary function. The death of Marja Gavrilovna's father is also ultimately unimportant to the plot. When she meets Burmin, their happiness is not clouded by the memory of the tragic consequences of his wild prank in the church in Žadrino, and the tale ends on a note of joy.

"Mistress into Maid" lacks pathos, and the entire tale brims with happiness, but death rears its head here as well. Both landowners, Berestov and Muromskij, are widowers. The deaths of their wives are described only in passing, however. Berestov's wife died in childbirth while he was away hunting, and it is stated that Muromskij "having squandered the greater part of his fortune in Moscow and having become a widower, retired to his sole remaining estate. . . ."[24] The two neighbors are, it seems, merry widowers who apparently wasted no tears over their deceased spouses.

The theme of widowhood is found in all five tales and in Variant II tends to evolve in the same way as the theme of death. Samson Vyrin is a widower who treasures the memory of his wife as he gazes with sadness at his beautiful daughter: ". . . such a bright girl, so quick, just like her late mother."[25] Vyrin's lonely death is even sadder in light of his widowerhood. In "The Shot" the Countess is threatened with widowhood as a result of Silvio's unsolicited visit to her husband's estate. The protagonist in "The Undertaker" is a widower, though the fact, as such, is not mentioned. In "The Snowstorm" a complex situation revolving around the pseudo-widowhood and the separation of the wedded couple is abruptly and happily resolved at the end of the tale. Finally in "Mistress into Maid" widowerhood has obviously not cast a shadow over the lives of the two landowners. There is thus a conscious gradation of emotion and theme in the tales in Variant II following an ascending curve from pathos to joy. Within this system "The Stationmaster" and "Mistress into Maid" represent trough and peak respectively.

That the cycle focuses on the problem of inner freedom versus self-enslavement is supported by the presentation of the upper and lower classes alternately in the tales in Variant II. In Variant I the editor, A.P., destroyed this alternation; he placed the two tales dealing primarily with the nobility at the beginning of the cycle and followed them with the two depicting the life of the lower classes. Variant II, however, begins with a tale from lower-class life narrated by a nobleman whose sympathies lie with the stationmaster and his daughter Dunja. This speaks as eloquently for the manner in which different social classes are presented as does the actual sequence of the tales. In Variant II, "The Shot" immediately follows "The Stationmaster." The order here clearly suggests the theme of the cycle. The self-enslavement of the narrator, I.L.P., stands in bold contrast to the inner freedom of his counterpart, A.G.N., and thus prompts the "curious researcher" to compare the two. The remaining tales restate the theme of inner freedom illustrated by different social strata with "Mistress into Maid" providing a fitting conclusion with its repeated disregard of class barriers as reflected even in the title of the tale.

In Variant II optimism and lightheartedness slowly build to a peak in the last tale. The second part of "The Snowstorm," immediately preceding "Mistress into Maid" is infused with the atmosphere of national triumph characteristic of the period at the end of the Napoleonic war:

> Officers who had left for the campaign as mere fellows returned as grown men, matured by the air of the battlefield and with crosses on their uniforms. Soldiers chatted gaily with one another, constantly mixing French and German words in their speech. An unforgettable time! A time of glory and enthusiasm! How strongly the Russian heart beat at the word *fatherland!* How sweet were the tears of reunion! With what common feeling we combined our sense of national pride with love for the tsar! And what a moment it was for him![26]

The joyous note on which the cycle ends begins from the moment the army returns in "The Snowstorm." It is at this point that the riddle of the tale begins to unravel. Marja Gavrilovna's bad dream, reminiscent to a certain extent of the undertaker's nightmare, recedes into the past; the death of Vladimir, in some respects parallel to Vyrin's except that it casts no gloom over the happiness awaiting the couple, is forgotten; Burmin's prank, redolent of Minskij's abduction in "The Stationmaster," is resolved happily. 1815, the year of the army's triumphant return from Western Europe, marks the turning point in the story and strikes the first note of joy upon which "The Snowstorm" ends. This mood dominates the following tale, "Mistress into Maid," as well and the end of the entire cycle.

The role the foreign campaign played in the history of Russia, how it influenced the cream of Russian nobility, and the nature of the link between this campaign and the future Decembrists' concern with freedom are well known. Soon after 1815 these young free thinkers began to meet:

> They had their meetings,
> And over a cup of wine,
> And over Russian vodka
>
> 27

Puškin writes in the burned and coded tenth chapter of *Eugene Onegin*.

> Renowned for harsh rhetoric,
> The members of this family met
> At restless Nikita's,
> At cautious Il'ja's.[28]
>
> ....
>
> At first these conspiracies [discussed]
> Over Lafitte and Cliqueau
> Were only friendly quarrels,
> And the science of rebellion did not penetrate
> Their hearts very deeply.
> It was all only boredom,
> The idleness of young minds,
> The amusements of adult pranksters[29]
>
> ....

It is significant that on the manuscript of "The Snowstorm," Puškin left a note about burning this chapter of *Eugene Onegin*.[30]

A decade of hopes, bold schemes, and plans commenced from the year 1815. It was as if the young thinkers among the nobility shook off the burden of the past and strove forward into the future. Puškin's switch to a new structural scheme in the middle of "The Snowstorm" reflects this change. Beginning with the description of 1815, the tale no longer focuses on the past but on the future: Vladimir's death is overshadowed by the expectation of the resolution of Burmin's courtship. All of "Mistress into Maid," likewise, is oriented toward the future. Its plot in no way revolves around events that have occurred in the past. Exactly the opposite is characteristic of "The Stationmaster," "The Shot," "The Undertaker" and the first half of "The Snowstorm." Thus the very structure of the cycle generates new hope and expectations.[31]

In Variant II, "The Snowstorm" with its portentous date of 1815 precedes "Mistress into Maid." The latter, in a sense, extends the emotional line of the second part of "The Snowstorm," as well as forms the peak of the entire cycle and interacts with the introduction to "The Stationmaster" and the liberal remarks of the Titular Counsellor A.G.N.

Footnotes

1. P. v. 8, I, p. 97 (4-9).
2. Ibid., p. 98 (11-14).
3. Ibid., (15).
4. Ibid., (16).
5. Ibid., p. 97(1).
6. Ibid., p. 98 (20).
7. Ibid., (23-24).
8. Ibid., p. 459 (27).
9. Ibid., p. 98 (24).
10. Ibid., (27).
11. Ibid.
12. Ibid., II, p. 642 (27-28).
13. Ibid., I, p. 98 (28).
14. Ibid.
15. Ibid., (8).
16. Ibid., v. 11, p. 44 (7-12).
17. Ibid., (18-23).
18. Ibid., v. 8, II, p. 641 (24-27).
19. Ibid., v. 13, p. 315 (Letter dated Dec. 23, 1926).
20. P., v. 8, I, p. 98 (27-28).
21. Ibid. (8-10).
22. Ibid., p. 68 (34).
23. Ibid., p. 74 (36).
24. Ibid., p. 109 (17-19).
25. Ibid., p. 98 (38-39).
26. Ibid., p. 83 (12-19).
27. Ibid., v. 6, p. 523, stanza 13.
28. Ibid., stanza 14.
29. Ibid., p. 525, stanza 17.
30. Ibid., p. 526 and P., v. 8, II, p. 622.
31. The orientation of "Mistress into Maid" toward the future is emphasized by a foreshadowing of the denouement. The address of Alexej's letter, which becomes known to the local young ladies, reads as follows: "To Akulina Petrovna Kuročkina in Moscow, opposite the Alexeevskij Monastery, in the house of the coppersmith Savel'ev, with a respectful request to deliver this letter to A.N.R." (P., v. 8, I, p. 110 (27-30)). In the last scene of the story Alexej finds Liza reading his letter which was originally sent to Akulina, the daughter of a blacksmith, and which eventually finds its way to the daughter of a landowner. P., v. 8, I, p. 123 (37-40).

CHAPTER 2

BELKIN'S AUTOBIOGRAPHICAL TALES

The contrast repeatedly drawn between two characters—one free from, the other enslaved by social and cultural dictates—first appears in the foreword in the neighbor's biography of the fictitious author of the tales. Here a benevolent, yet calculating and shrewd landowner stands in contrast to Ivan Petrovič, a writer and dreamer who neglects the management of his estate. Belkin's seemingly carefree and lighthearted attitude distinguishes him from his neighbor who is incapable of understanding Belkin's indifference to the philistine details of everyday existence that are so important to the author of the letter. Accordingly, the most vivid part of the letter is that in which Belkin pretends to fall asleep while the neighbor interrogates the village elder. Also contributing to the antithesis is the neighbor's reluctance to be associated with men of letters. The seed of the antithesis that characterizes the entire cycle is thus planted in Belkin's biography. His five tales reflect in their structure the conflict between Belkin and his neighbor.

The autobiographical quality of Belkin's tales is reflected in the basic problems treated therein and closely parallels his neighbor's letter. Belkin's first four tales deal with conflicts based on various human values or prejudices. "The Stationmaster" exposes the conflict between generations: a father's misunderstanding of his daughter and her struggle for independent self-fulfillment. The conflict in "The Shot" is precipitated by the intrusion of an outsider who shakes the established order. In fact, this situation occurs in this tale three times: first, a new young officer, R***, does not accept Silvio's authority at the gambling table; then in Silvio's narrative the same role is played by the young Count in Silvio's regiment; and, finally, Silvio himself appears authoritatively without invitation at the Count's estate. In "The Undertaker" the conflict is based on the professional isolation of Adrijan, who feels estranged from other craftsmen and compares his occupation with the other lonely ones of hangman and jester. In the fourth tale, "The Snowstorm," a love story, the conflict is spiced with false romantic assumptions, an act of Providence (the snowstorm), and Burmin's unpredictable prank.

Curiously, an identical set of human beliefs, prejudices, and misconceptions with potential conflicts is found in the neighbor's letter in the foreword. At this point reference will be made to paragraphs IV to VII according to the presentation of this text in Chapter I. These four paragraphs of the neighbor's letter describe Belkin's life at his estate where his tales were written.

The first direct mention of the clash between two different world views comes at the beginning of paragraph IV:

> After assuming the management of his estate, Ivan Petrovič soon began to neglect the household affairs because of his inexperience and softheartedness and relaxed the strict order established by his late parent.

There follows a risible account of how Ivan Petrovič replaced the efficient village elder with one elected by his serfs, and for corvée substituted quit-rent, payable by the peasants in the form of cranberries and nuts—token payment at best.

Between the two landowners, Belkin and his neighbor, there was a strong undercurrent of hostility that easily could have erupted into direct confrontation. The foreword, however, not only juxtaposes Belkin to his neighbor but also suggests a conflict between Belkin and his late father with whom the neighbor is associated: "As a friend of Ivan Petrovič's late parent, I considered it my duty to offer my advice to his son also . . ." (IV). So the neighbor had given managerial advice to Belkin's father of whom, from all appearances, he approved: "He was not a wealthy man but was moderate and extremely shrewd in business matters" (III). Thus, through the neighbor's criticism of Belkin one can surmise what Belkin's late father's attitude would have been toward his son's lifestyle and mismanagement of the estate. The conflict then was not simply one between neighbors; it was a broader one between generations.

One of the reasons for this generation gap was the inflexible attitude of the older generation towards one's function in society. Belkin's neighbor, as very likely Belkin's late father, considered that a landowner's duty was to run his estate strictly and authoritatively, to keep his serfs in their proper place, and to reap as much profit as possible. This attitude may be inferred in the neighbor's letter which, while addressed to the editor of the tales, deals only superficially with Belkin as a writer and is more concerned with Belkin's poor handling of his estate. The neighbor refuses to acknowledge the importance of Belkin's avocation and passion for writing. A total lack of understanding of the essence of another human being characterizes the neighbor's attitude toward Belkin and, by extension, the relationship between Belkin and his father.

One may discover this same attitude in Samson Vyrin's love for his daughter, Dunja. During the narrator, A.G.N.'s first visit he considers

Dunja a coquette. He notes his impressions of her beauty and of the kiss she allows him before his departure. Her father, however, only thinks she is "so bright and so quick—just like her late mother."[1] During A.G.N.'s second visit to the station Vyrin's utilitarian evaluation of his daughter is clarified at the beginning of his long account of Dunja's elopement and his misfortune. There is, of course, good reason for such a simplistic misrepresentation of Dunja. It reflects the traditional way of life and thinking of the peasant class. Similarly, as seen in paragraph IV of the letter to the editor, the neighbor's traditional thinking and perceptions lead him to ignore Belkin's gift for writing, thus paralleling Vyrin's attitude toward Dunja.

In paragraph V of the neighbor's letter another aspect of his relationship with Belkin comes to the fore. The neighbor, with fatherly concern for the son of his late friend, insists on advising Belkin on managing his estate. Even if relations between the neighbors were genuinely friendly, it would have been highly irregular simply to arrive at Gorjuxino in order to inspect the estate accounts as if they were one's own property. This would be an unheard-of intrusion into the sphere of someone else's authority. But Belkin, feigning disinterest and naiveté, rather than have a confrontation, prefers to fall asleep on a chair during the interrogation which was likely conducted in a loud voice and, perhaps, even accompanied by the pounding of fists on a table. One may well assume, of course, that the reason for Belkin's pretense of sleep is his desire to escape the embarrassment of such a head-on confrontation. Belkin is infinitely more eager to feign managerial ineptness than to publicize his *de facto* emancipation of his serfs by refusing to live off their labor. Similarly in "The Shot" a man, superior in certain respects to the one originally wielding hegemony, also intrudes without malice, but the result is an open confrontation between Silvio and the Count. Belkin avoids such a clash simply by pretending to be asleep.

The anticlimax that follows the neighbor's interrogation of the village-elder is also paralleled in the first chapter of "The Shot." There is a lexical link between the fifth paragraph of the neighbor's letter and the description of Silvio's keeping bank during the card game in his house. In both passages the word *"xozjajstvennyj"* (household, adj.) or *"xozjajničat'"* (to manage) occurs. In the letter it is used concretely: *"Dlja sego, priexav odnaždy k nemu, potreboval ja xozjajstvennye knigi . . ."* (V); *"S tex por perestal ja vmešivat'sja v ego xozjajstvennye rasporjaženija . . ."* (V) ("For this purpose, having arrived one day at his estate, I demanded the account (management) books, . . ." (V); "thereafter I ceased to interfere in his actions regarding the management . . ." (V)). In "The Shot," *"xozjajničat'"* is used metaphorically: *"My už èto znali i ne mešali emu xozjajničat' posvoemu"* ("We were all aware of this and made no attempt to interfere with his management").[2] In both cases the established order of *"xozjajstvo"* (household or management) is challenged by an outsider. In "The Shot" it is the new officer, R***, who insults Silvio. All the officers expect a duel between Silvio and R***, who objects to a custom instituted by Silvio in his own home. It is Silvio's decision, however, not to fight this duel, because of the pre-eminence of another unresolved conflict, i.e. the duel with the Count, who six years before was also an intruder in the regiment in which Silvio enjoyed prestige and authority. Silvio's reaction to the Count's intrusion contrasts sharply with Belkin's reaction to his neighbor's intrusion and attempted management of his estate.

It must not be forgotten that in the introduction Belkin and his neighbor constantly stand on the precipice of open antagonism. One has only to read the beginning of paragraph VI:

> Our friendly relations, however, were by no means impaired by all this because, while deploring his weakness and that sort of ruinous neglect which is common nowadays among our young gentry, I had a sincere liking for Ivan Petrovič.

The neighbor, in his naiveté, cannot distinguish Belkin's pretenses from his inability to conduct his affairs, or his deliberate economic emancipation of his serfs from carelessness and capriciousness. Harmony between the neighbors is preserved only through Belkin's wisdom and his indifference to personal prestige and authority. The neighbor's "sincere liking for Ivan Petrovič" is not the real reason for peace between the neighbors.

The neighbor's misinterpretation of events allows Puškin to introduce a new detail into Ivan Petrovič's life: his utter loneliness and isolation. The letter evidences the fact that Belkin was respectful of his neighbor. "He valued my [his neighbor's] simple conversation although in habits, manner of thinking, and disposition" (VI) they had nothing in common, according to the neighbor. Beneath the smooth flow of the neighbor's style lies a paradox. Indeed, what kind of friendship and mutual attachment could there be between two men who share nothing intellectually, emotionally, or socially? Thus the sixth paragraph of the neighbor's letter exposes the hypocrisy of the relationship he imposed on Belkin and the latter's loneliness, the most painful burden he endures while at his estate.

In a grotesque form an imposed relationship also occurs in "The Undertaker" at the climax of Adrijan's nightmare:

At this moment a small skeleton pushed its way through the crowd and approached Adrijan. . . . "You do not recognize me, Proxorov," said the skeleton. . . . With these words the skeleton stretched out its arms in a bony embrace, but Adrijan, mustering up all his strength, shrieked and pushed it away.[3]

Bear in mind that this scene allegedly was written by a lonely man required to show respect to a neighbor who thrust his friendship upon him despite the fact that they had absolutely nothing in common. This is analogous to Adrijan's relations with his fellow craftsmen as well as the corpses with whom he has no common meeting ground other than their Russian nationality and orthodoxy. Moreover, the neighbor represents for Belkin an obsolete order, which should have been buried long ago.

There is an additional link between paragraph VI of the neighbor's letter and "The Undertaker." The differences between the two neighbors may be ascribed to Belkin's inclination toward meditation and art and his neighbor's philistinism. Belkin's loneliness was the loneliness of an artist. In "The Undertaker," Proxorov, while cursing the German craftsmen, tries to convince himself that his occupation is not dishonorable. The professions to which he refers, are, like his, rather lonely or disparaged: "What is it, really . . . ? Is my trade less honorable than others? Is an undertaker brother to a hangman? . . . Is an undertaker a carnival jester?"[4] To this list of professions priest, prophet, and artist might be added. Proxorov, of course, would not have grasped the relationship between undertaker and poet, but in his drunken mutterings he touches upon the crux of the problem in naming professions which by their nature stand apart and whose representatives—priests, poets, prophets, jesters, hangmen and undertakers—are ostracized. Just as poets and undertakers are pariahs, so are Belkin and Proxorov.

Paragraph VII adds yet another stroke to the portrait of Belkin: "He had a great inclination towards the opposite sex but in fact was as bashful as a young girl." Why did Puškin introduce Belkin's attitude toward women? To answer this question, one should keep in mind that the name of the neighbor's village, Nenaradovo, is mentioned in "The Snowstorm" and is confirmed by the neighbor himself:

The names of almost all the characters, however, are fictitious; those of the hamlets and villages have been borrowed from this district, my own village being mentioned somewhere. This was not through some kind of wicked intention, but merely lack of imagination (VIII).

In this passage an important detail must not go unnoticed: the neighbor, speaking of the name of his estate borrowed by Belkin, cannot help but be on the defensive. He emphasizes that Belkin did not have any wicked intention in doing so. In a letter that, as has been shown already, misrepresents almost every detail described, such a defensive posture very well may indicate that Belkin had some reason to ridicule the inhabitants of Nenaradovo in "The Snowstorm." It also may be concluded that in this story the contrast between the two estates is drawn from reality: Nenaradovo, the residence of a conservative, well-to-do family with a debutante daughter, and a neighboring estate, suggesting Gorjuxino, owned by a young bachelor of meager means.

One further connection between the sixth paragraph of the foreword with "The Snowstorm" may be made, and that is A.P.'s first footnote. Although, as has been demonstrated already, both of the editor's footnotes to the neighbor's letter play a crucial role in Puškin's code, the first fulfills still another function in alluding to the fact that this paragraph originally contained a certain humorous anecdote that A.P. deleted. The content of the paragraph clearly indicates that the anecdote deals with Belkin's relationship with a lady.

"The Snowstorm" is the sole tale dealing comically with the failure of a love affair, and, therefore, possibly hints at one of Belkin's own romances. Both liaisons are marked by failure. Neither "The Shot" nor "The Stationmaster" reflects a comparable situation. In "The Undertaker" there is no romance, and in "Mistress into Maid" misfortune is totally alien to the story. Therefore, it is only in "The Snowstorm," and then only in that part of the tale dealing with Vladimir, that there is the suggestion of the anecdote about Belkin deleted from the neighbor's letter by A.P. Belkin well may have found himself in a humorous predicament, mention of which could contain "nothing injurious to the memory" (VIII) of the hero.

In summary, the four paragraphs of the neighbor's letter mentioned above related to the four tales as follows: Paragraph IV relates to "The Stationmaster"; paragraph V, to "The Shot"; paragraph VI, to "The Undertaker"; and paragraph VII, to "The Snowstorm." Had the tales been published in the above-indicated order, the interrelationship between them and the four paragraphs of the introduction would have been more apparent. Puškin left a clue, however, that is extremely important for a definitive analysis of his work: the sequence of tales as they appear in Belkin's manuscript—Variant II. This sequence enables one to relate the tales to Belkin's biography, to perceive them as autobiographical notes on problems he confronted, thus turning the entire work into an artistic whole with a single protagonist, I. P. Belkin.

Since the order of the tales in Belkin's manuscript reflects the order in which they were written, one may hypothesize that the tales were an outgrowth of personal problems that Belkin had to face on his estate. After his arrival and first managerial decisions he no doubt felt strong disapproval from his neighbor, the friend of his late father. This situation could have reminded Belkin of a story told to him some time ago by Titular Counsellor A.G.N., in which the older generation cannot admit the possibility of the younger living by its own reason. The parable of the prodigal son links these two settings of biography and fiction. After having avoided a direct confrontation with his neighbor by simulating total managerial incompetence, Belkin could have thought of another story about a prolonged duel triggered by an unwarranted intrusion. Loneliness at his estate might have suggested to Belkin a story about an undertaker who felt like an outcast at a party attended by other craftsmen. Perhaps Belkin's reflections on his own loneliness prompted him to find a sweetheart, but some humorous event foiled his attempt to marry. This episode remains unknown to us, for the editor, A.P., has deleted it from the neighbor's letter, but Belkin himself may have recollected a story told to him by a young lady, demoiselle K.I.T., about an amorous adventure ending with a humorous twist. Belkin entitled this story "The Snowstorm" and concluded his cycle with another tale told by the same young lady which he called "Mistress into Maid."

If one accepts this hypothesis, another observation may be made, namely, that Belkin was compelled to write his tales by some painful circumstances in his life, circumstances externally imposed on him. While projecting his own experiences on the screen of fiction, Belkin, however, granted his characters escapes from their predicaments, liberating them from circumstances similar to those that trapped him on his estate at Gorjuxino. The toponym itself suggests grief in Russian from the root, *gore*. This might be the reason that the first four of Belkin's tales contain a common denominator—the confrontation of two philosophies with a resulting unconventional triumph—and also for a utopian story, "Mistress into Maid," at the end. For Belkin it seems to be an artistic escape from his eluctable reality. The autobiographical flavor of Belkin's tales must have stimulated the otherwise inexplicable exclamation of a reviewer in *The Northern Bee*: "Everywhere is Belkin and Belkin! The reader wants tales and not Belkin."[5]

Footnotes

1. P. v. 8, p. 98 (38).
2. Ibid., p. 66 (15).
3. Ibid., p. 93 (38).
4. Ibid., p. 92 (13).
5. P. N. Stolpanskij, "Puškin i 'Severnaja pčela,'" *Puškin i ego sovremenniki*, Petrograd, 1914, XIX-XX, p. 160.

CHAPTER 3

THE STRUCTURE

The interrelation between the editor's foreword and the following five tales can also be examined from another vantage point, i.e. as Puškin's creation. In this case the entire text of six tales must be viewed as one artistic entity reflecting the narrative strategy of the actual author, Alexander Puškin. Besides Puškin's attempt to leave a record, disguised as fiction, related to the Decembrist movement he experimented with basic narrative structures and created a narrative model of stories containing a mystery in his first accomplished work of prose. It has already been established that the five *Tales of Belkin* can, to a certain extent, be classified as mystery stories with rather subtle suspense sustained throughout each. As soon as the curiosity of the puzzled person had been satisfied, Puškin put down his pen.[1]

Every mystery provokes curiosity which may be directed either into the past or the future. All five tales of Belkin are based on a mystery arousing curiosity directed into the past. In other words, the person Puškin chooses to puzzle and confuse in each story finds himself confronting a situation unexplained by available facts. New information must be added to shed light on the past in order to elucidate the present. The puzzled person does not inquire about the future, "What will come next?" or "How will this situation be resolved?" but rather "Why?" or "How did this situation come about?" His questions concern past events and have to be answered in the past tense. The basic question in each of the five tales confirms this point: 1.) "The Stationmaster": What was Dunja's fate in St. Petersburg?; 2.) "The Shot": What was the outcome of Silvio's duel?; 3.) "The Undertaker": When did Adrijan's dream begin?; and 4.) "The Snowstorm": What happened in the church? 5.) "Mistress into Maid" represents a dual situation: while the reader is fully informed of all of Lisa's pranks and disguises, he still remains curious about the outcome of this intrigue. Alexej, however, being totally unaware of the existence of any mystery at the beginning of the tale must, at the denouement, ask himself the question: How did it happen that two different girls turned into a new one, the real Lisa?

It is thus not only the reader who confronts a mystery and whose curiosity is consequently aroused. The mystified participants may be: 1.) the characters as well as the reader, but not the narrator ("The Undertaker" and "The Snowstorm"); 2.) the narrator and the reader ("The

78

Stationmaster" and "The Shot"); 3.) one character only ("Mistress into Maid"). To this list may be added the sixth tale, "From the Editor," which presents a mystery not to the general readers but only to the "curious researchers," as designated by the editor, A.P.

One may regard a mystery and its solution as the basic structural element in Puškin's collection of six tales. However, they are diversified by a variety of methods by which the mystery is introduced and solved. The six tales can be divided into two categories: three stories told in the first person by a narrator who participates in the plot of the story and three tales told in the third person with an omniscient narrator. The first category contains the foreword, "From the Editor," narrated by A.P.; "The Stationmaster," narrated by A.G.N.; and "The Shot," narrated by I.L.P. These three narrators elicit some kind of information concerning an event or situation which needs clarification. The editor, A.P., contacts Belkin's neighbor allegedly to satisfy the reader's curiosity about the author of the five tales; A.G.N. provokes the stationmaster into telling the story of his daughter and makes an extra effort to visit the station a third time to discover the outcome of Dunja's adventure; I.L.P. learns of the result of Silvio's duel and his death. The second set of tales, consisting of "The Undertaker," "The Snowstorm," and "Mistress into Maid," has a third-person, omniscient narrator. The narrator in the first set of tales seeks the solution of a mystery while in the second set the narrator is the primary agent of the mystery.

The methods of solving the mysteries also function as diversifying elements in the entire cycle of six tales. The best examples of this diversity are found in "The Stationmaster," "The Shot," "The Undertaker," and "The Snowstorm." These four contain distinctive variants which together form a system. The final bit of information needed for answering the question of Dunja's fate in St. Petersburg is given to the narrator, A.G.N., by the boy. In "The Shot" there are two mysteries: why did Silvio avoid the duel with R*** in the first chapter, and what was the outcome of Silvio's duel with the Count in the second chapter? Both mysteries are solved by the accounts given by two characters to the narrator, I.L.P. In "The Undertaker" the question as to when Adrijan's dream began is answered by the servant's statement to the protagonist, Proxorov. In "The Snowstorm" two questions—What happened in the Žadrino church, and whom did Burmin marry in an unknown village? —are resolved by exchanges of information between two characters, Burmin and Marja Gavrilovna.

One can detect a different, though complementary, structure in the two remaining tales, "Mistress into Maid," and "From the Editor." In the former the narrator and the reader are aware of Lisa's pranks and, consequently, participate, albeit passively, in the conspiracy against Alexej. At the denouement of the tale Alexej simultaneously discovers the mystery and its solution, without any verbal explanation. A certain similarity to this structure is apparent in the foreword, "From the Editor." In this case the mystified party is the reader, although he is at first unaware of a mystery. But as soon as one reads the story and finds the questionable dating of the neighbor's letter (XII, 31), one may begin to re-examine the entire tale and find the inconsistency in the editor's remarks regarding changes in, or footnotes to, the letter (I, 4; VII, 19; VIII, 24). Growing increasingly suspicious, the reader may suspect a code and become a "curious researcher" (VIII, 25). Eventually the researcher may break the code and solve both mysteries of the tale, Belkin's biography and the fate of his manuscript. As soon as the reader begins to investigate, he assumes the role of a character in the story, since he begins to act exactly as prescribed by the author, Puškin, by fulfilling an essential function without which the plot of the tale remains unrealized. The solution of the mysteries in "From the Editor," however, can only be arrived at by witnessing the events, registering all the details, ordering them and drawing the right conclusions. In a sense this process is identical to that which takes place in Alexej's mind at the denouement of "Mistress into Maid." The only distinction between these two solutions lies in the complexity of the code in "From the Editor" and the simplicity of the puzzle in "Mistress into Maid."

A mystery is central to each of the six tales structured according to the following narrative elements which unify the tales while providing diversity:

1) the participation of the narrator in the plot (as a narrator and a character or as an omniscient narrator):

2) the grammatical person of the narration (first or third person);

3) the number of mysteries (always one major mystery but a secondary one as well in some stories);

4) the nature of the solution of the mystery (verbal or not, implied or direct);

5) the number of participants in the solution of the mystery (in some stories, one; in others, two or none);

6) the recipient of the information solving the mystery (the narrator, a character or the reader).

The following Chart A demonstrates the interrelation of these narrative elements with the narrator designated by N; the characters, by C; the mystery and the mystification of the particular participant by M; and the course the verbal solution of the mystery takes, by an arrow.

Chart A	1. Participating N 2. First-person N 3. 2 M		1. Non-participating omniscient N 2. Third-person N 3. 1 M		
4. Implied verbal solution of M		*"The Stationmaster"* (CM) (NM) ⟶ (RM) ↖ C	*"The Undertaker"* C N ↓⟶ (RM) (CM)		5. M unveiled by 1 individual
4. Analytical perception of solution of M	*"From the Editor"* C N (RM) C			*"Mistress into Maid"* (CM) N R C	5. M unveiled by 0 individuals
4. Direct verbal solution of M		*"The Shot"* C ↙ (NM) ⟶ (RM) ↖ C	*"The Snowstorm"* (CM) N ↑⟶ (RM) (CM)		5. M unveiled by 2 individuals
	6. The recipient is R.	6. The recipients are N and R.	6. The recipients are C and R.	6. The recipient is C.	

Chart A demonstrates the remarkable consistency with which Puškin carried out his narrative structure in the six tales. The point of this system is that it is based on a limited number of elements which do recur in various combinations, most of them being repeated only twice, but in every instance combined with different elements. The result is an extremely tight structural unity with remarkable versatility. The most revealing observation for the present study, however, is the fact that the tale, "From the Editor," is perfectly integrated in terms of narrative structure in the Puškin cycle. "From the Editor" complements the structural interrelation of the five tales and is linked to the final tale, "Mistress into Maid." This interaction results in a perfectly symmetrical cycle, as complementary tales are placed at both extremes. In both tales the non-verbal solution of the central mystery is achieved by analytical reevaluation of the available facts, and in both tales the mystery is rendered by means of some sort of disguise. Lisa's simple masquerade is paralleled in the tale, "From the Editor," by Belkin's simulated managerial incapacity and feeblemindedness.

Finally, one may conclude that the narrative structure of the entire cycle blends perfectly with its philosophical content. On both levels a mystery occupies the central position, and the reader's penetration beneath a deceptively smooth surface is one of the major components of the plot. Just as Alexej's understanding of Lisa's intrigue is an indispensable component of the plot of "Mistress into Maid," so is the decoding by the "curious researcher" an integral part of the plot developed in the foreword, "From the Editor." By reevaluating I. P. Belkin's biography and personality, the "curious researcher" establishes the autobiographical flavor of all of Belkin's five stories.

One point remains to be clarified: whether the number of tales is arbitrary. Since Puškin exhausted the available types of interrelations among a limited number of narrative elements in this mystery cycle it remains to examine Puškin's narrative model in the framework of all theoretically possible combinations.

It seems that Puškin limited himself to two variables in structuring the mysteries: mystification or awareness of the mystery and the number of participants among whom the mystification could be distributed in various ways. These participants are four, the narrator, the reader, and two characters. Although all the tales in Puškin's cycle have more than two characters, at the end of each tale only two are present either physically or by implication, and both of them are directly involved in the mystery and its solution. Thus in each tale there are four participants related to the mystery. This number of participants allows theoretically

16 different relationships to the mystery. In the following Chart B the mystification of a participant is indicated by M:

Chart B

	1	2	3	4	5	6	7	8	9	10	11	12	13	14	15	16
R	M	M	M	M	M			M	M							M
N		M	M					M			M	M	M	M		M
C			M		M		M		M	M	M	M				M
C				M	M	M	M	M			M		M			M

The last two versions, 15 and 16, must be discarded as inapplicable in the ordinary narrative, for 15 does not contain any mystery, and in 16 no one can provide the solution to the mystery. Numbers 11, 12, 13, 14 must be eliminated for the simple reason that a mystery story with an informed reader and a mystified narrator is unlikely to appear except in a highly experimental narrative. Redundance of certain versions demands further eliminations: 10 actually repeats 6, since both contain only one mystified character; 9 repeats 4, since in both cases only the reader and one character are mystified; 8 repeats 3, since in both the mystified participants are the reader, the narrator and one character; 7 repeats 6 and 10, since in all cases only characters are mystified while the narrator and the reader are not. In fact $7 = 6 + 10$. Since 10 numbers (7-16) are eliminated, only 6 (1-6) remain to be compared with the six tales of Puškin in question. It appears, as shown in Chart C, that this set of six narrative schemes coincides with Puškin's narrative strategy:

Chart C

	R	N	C	C
1. "From the Editor"	M			
2. "The Shot"	M	M		
3. "The Stationmaster"	M	M	M	
4. "The Undertaker"	M			M
5. "The Snowstorm"	M		M	M
6. "Mistress into Maid"				M

In "From the Editor" the neighbor knows what to disclose and what to conceal in Belkin's biography. In addition, the concealed facts are perfectly known to A.P.; however, the reader, the "curious researcher," must discover them by himself. In "The Shot" only the narrator and the reader are mystified. In "The Stationmaster" the reader, the narrator and Vyrin are mystified (the little boy is unaware of the mystery). In "The Undertaker" the reader and Adrijan are mystified (the servant is unaware of the mystery). In "The Snowstorm" the reader and two protagonists are mystified. And in "Mistress into Maid" only Alexej is both unaware of and mystified by Lisa's prank. In the last three tales the narrator is omniscient and, consequently, is not mystified.

It appears that Puškin during the autumn of 1830 in Boldino was experimenting with several subjects simultaneously. He introduced into Russian literature a character (I. P. Belkin), affiliated with the Decembrist movement, created a complex code and built into six "mystery" stories a narrative model that exhausted all the reasonable narrative possibilities in Puškin's time.

Footnote

See: A. Ležnev, *Proza Puškina*, M., 1966, p. 177.

CHAPTER 4

PUŠKIN'S TALES AND HISTORY

In the course of this study the scope of *The Tales of Belkin* has gradually broadened. It is needless to reemphasize that it is not the individual tales that are at issue here but a work of much richer content more tightly unified into an artistic whole. A common plot unites the cycle, including the foreword, a reappraisal of which transforms the individual tales into component parts of Belkin's biography.

Each tale comes to be seen as an individual sign interacting with other signs within a complex, coded system. Puškin constructed one basic plot for the tales revolving around the nature of freedom in which the individual plots play a secondary role. The plot of the cycle is incomparably broader than the tales themselves and centers around the fictional author, Belkin, as the protagonist.

With rare historical scope and precision Puškin reflects his own era in this work. He introduces the tales in such a way that his "researcher" is compelled to consider them in light of the biographical information furnished about Belkin. Furthermore, Belkin's life could not be apprehended clearly without a clarification of the role of the editor and without an investigation of the way in which Belkin's manuscript reached the editor. All the signs contribute to the work to a greater or lesser degree, supplement, and illuminate one another. From them a vivid picture of Russia in the 1820's gradually emerges.

At first glance the tales seem to reflect the liveliness of Alexander I's reign with duels between hussar officers, light-heartedness and merriment, officers marrying strange women without a thought or Imperial Guard officers falling in love with daughters of stationmasters and carrying them off. The epoch of Alexander is reflected here historically as well: "The Undertaker" is set against the background of Moscow as it was rebuilt after the fire of 1812; it is in Moscow that Vladimir dies in "The Snowstorm" on the eve of Napoleon's entrance, and the same story contains a passage about the general enthusiasm and the glorious days after the victory of 1815.

But beneath the obvious historical references lie the internal contra-

85

dictions of the tales that revolve around the solitary meditations of Belkin, a freethinking landowner. The very fact that the theme of the tales has remained hidden is ample evidence of the political climate of that era when one's thoughts on freedom could be expressed only under the guise of entertaining anecdotes. The fictitious author of these stories proceeded to liberate the peasants of his estate as if in anticipation of the national reform of the serf system, a reform that the new forces arising and gathering strength from 1815 on would attempt to effect. Belkin, in keeping with his coded biography, feigned the simpleton but was undoubtedly in contact with his fellow freethinkers whom he met in the 32nd Jäger infantry regiment and from whom he must have received the handwritten copy of Griboedov's comedy, *Woe from Wit,* as Puškin himself received it from his Decembrist friend, I. Puščin. Not long before the uprising of December 14, Belkin presumably sent the manuscript of the tales to his liberal friend for publication. Soon after that, the revolt occurred followed by an investigation of all the insurgents and repression. A new era, that of Nicholas I, was born in Russia. For four years during this time (1826-1830) Belkin's manuscript remained with his friend who was presumably investigated in connection with the Decembrist affair since his name could not be revealed by A.P. (I). Belkin continued to write after December 14 but did not submit anything for publication and, moreover, made no arrangements for his manuscripts before his death (VIII). His liberal friend gave the manuscript to the editor, A.P., who "undertook the struggle" (I) over its publication. Realizing, however, that it would not pass the censor, he drew a veil over the tales: he destroyed their arrangement but made it possible for the "curious researcher" (VIII) to reconstruct the original order. For the sake of his own safety the editor underscored the authenticity of Belkin's authorship by printing the neighbor's letter (I).

The entire epoch in which Puškin lived permeates the tales. Alexander's Russia is depicted through the coded information about Belkin's military service (III). The political climate of the era of Nicholas is suggested in the foreword in the description of the fate of Belkin's manuscript and the history of its publication (I). Between the two eras lies an abyss; it is only felt, not expressed—a zero sign that eloquently betokens the fact that the Decembrist uprising could not be mentioned.

The Tales of Belkin consist of two sections reflecting two different eras: the foreword recounting that of Nicholas I precedes the second part, which is composed of five tales set during the reign of Alexander I. The second section can be understood accurately by the thoughtful reader although it requires long and careful examination; the first part concerned with Nicholas' rule is written as if with invisible ink, is coded by the editor, A.P., and demands not only thoughtful reading but exhaustive analysis by the "curious researcher." This contrast drawn by Puškin is itself a historical sketch. The atmosphere of the two eras was different; the changes that occurred were for the worse. Puškin does not depict them explicitly but introduces them dramatically in A.P.'s foreword to the tales. The manipulations, devices, and contrivances of the editor, A.P., are an intrinsic part of the plan of the work.

The reader must reread and reevaluate what he has read in the light of new observations. The reading of the whole all at once is required. Its complexity is reflected partially in the interrelationship of the characters in the foreword; they appear, disappear, or sometimes do not show themselves at all though they participate actively in the unfolding of events.

The fictitious history of the creation of the entire work, *The Tales of the Late I. P. Belkin*, proceeded gradually and necessitated the help of several characters. Presumably in the autumn of 1825 Ivan Petrovič Belkin completed the second part, the five tales. The neighbor mentions that in his house there were a great many manuscripts and that Belkin's housekeeper used the first part of a novel to paste up her windows (VIII 21). Furthermore, the neighbor says that the tales were Belkin's first literary effort (VIII, 22). Thus Belkin's literary production during the five years he spent in Gorjuxino was considerable. Since the tales were his first literary attempt, they pressumably took more time to write than the following works, but must have been finished by 1825. The first part, the foreword, was written by the editor five years later, in 1830. The integration of the two parts was left to unknown but aptly labeled characters—the "curious researchers." The characters in the first part are drawn obliquely and emerge only through the conscious efforts of these "curious researchers" after the publication of *The Tales*.

During the reign of Nicholas I all information about and references to the Decembrist plot or revolt were totally suppressed. This historical event was as if completely erased from the public's memory. Puškin's intention to write about the Decembrists as reflected in his remark of September 16, 1827, recorded in A. N. Vul'f's diary, is thus all the more astonishing:

> Puškin said while playing billiards: "I cannot comprehend how Karamzin could write in such a dry manner the first parts of his *History*, especially when writing about Igor' and Svjatoslav. This is the heroic period in our history. I shall *certainly* write the history of Peter I, and about Alexander I shall write with Kurbskij's pen. It is absolutely mandatory that we describe our contemporary events

so that in the future one could refer to us. It is already possible to write about the reign of Nicholas and about the 14th of December."[1]

Puškin's last phrase sounds like bravado unless it is considered in the context of *The Tales of Belkin*. Indeed, in 1830 Puškin kept his astonishing promise that he casually let drop during a game of billiards in 1827.

During his conversation with Vul'f, Puškin touched on other topics that later became significant in *The Tales of Belkin*, including Nicholas I's personal censorship and, most importantly, the note "On Popular Education" and the harsh criticism it had received. The significance of this note for understanding the introduction to "The Stationmaster" cannot, as has been shown, be overestimated. Thus, one may assume that Puškin conceived his historical work set during the reigns of Alexander and Nicholas sometime around September 16, 1827, at Mixajlovskoe, the estate where the author had previously spent two lonely years much as Belkin had passed the time in Gorjuxino.

The Tales of Belkin was indeed written with Kurbskij's brilliant and caustic pen under cover of the seemingly imbecilic Belkin, who by a ridiculous mistake has traditionally been identified with Mitrofan in Fonvizin's *The Minor*. Puškin himself doubtless with intention built this bridge between Ivan Belkin and Mitrofan Prostakov. The epigraph to the cycle of tales, an excerpt from Fonvizin's comedy, describes an improvised examination of the completely ignorant Mitrofan:

> Madam Prostakova: "That's so, my dear sir, he has been a lover of histories [tales] from his childhood."
> Skotinin: "Mitrofan has taken after me."

The remarks of the examiners preceding this passage are as follows:

> Pravdin: "Could not be better, he is very strong in grammar."
> Milon: "I hope he is as strong in history."[2]

Fonvizin's humor consists in reducing history to Mrs. Prostakova's "histories," or tales. Puškin in effect employs this pun in reverse. Instead of regressing from history to tales, he expects that his tales will be perceived on a higher level, that of history.

It may be that Puškin considered these tales which provide valid and critical commentary on his age a novel. In the same year that they were published Puškin wrote in his review of the novel, *Jurij Miloslavskij*, by M. Zagoskin: "In our time by the word 'novel' we mean a historical era developed within an invented narrative."[3] This makes no pretense of being a scholarly definition but is simply a formulation within the context of the review. Interestingly enough, the definition is a fitting one for *The Tales of Belkin*. Thus, perhaps Puškin did not compose separate tales in Boldino but rather wrote a historical novel in the pure sense of the word according to his definition, a novel that recounted the hopes and traumas of Russia in the 1820's and was published soon after this era ended.

Puškin's contemporaries and his critics, in general, grossly underrated the hero of the cycle. Puškin was apparently fond of Belkin, and the possibility that the latter ranked close in Puškin's estimate to Eugene Onegin, should not be overlooked. After all, Puškin introduced these protagonists similarly:

> Onegin, my good friend
> Was born on the banks of the Neva[4]

parallels Puškin's introduction of I. P. Belkin to Pletnev: "Recently I sent to you the tales of Belkin, my friend."[5]

Puškin's attachment to both these protagonists becomes all the more plausible in light of the fact that Belkin was created at the same time that Puškin burned the tenth chapter of his novel in verse in which the hero's destiny is presumably affected by the participants in the event intimated in A.P.'s foreword—the Decembrist revolt.

Footnotes

1. *A. S. Puškin v vospominanijax sovremennikov*, op. cit., 416.
2. *Pervoe i polnoe sobranie sočinenij D. I. Fonvizina*, St. Petersburg, 1888, p. 145.
3. First time appeared in *Literaturnaja gazeta* in January 1830. P., v. 11, pp. 92 5-6).
4. P., v. 6, p. 6.
5. P., v. 14, p. 189.

PART III

WRITING AND PUBLISHING

Chapter 1

THE TIME OF CONCEPTION

In studies of *The Tales of Belkin* scholars frequently pointed out that the foreword was not part of Puškin's original plan. Their claim was based in the author's own records dating the individual tales in the cycle and his correspondence with his friend and publisher, P.A. Pletnev. It is now generally accepted, however, that the foreword was written on September 14, thus during Puškin's work on his cycle. The manuscript of "The Undertaker" is dated September 9; "The Stationmaster," September 13, later corrected to September 14; "Mistress into Maid," September 20; "The Shot," October 14; and "The Snowstorm," October 20. "From the Editor" was completed on the same day as "The Stationmaster" and five days after "The Undertaker."[1]

A clear definition of the relationship between the figure of Belkin and the cycle of tales is possible only after the stories have been analyzed from the standpoint of the history of their artistic conception and actual writing. One must then attempt to probe further the prehistory of the actual writing of "The Tales of Belkin," to correlate the internal chronology of the individual tales with Belkin's fictional biography. In this respect "The Undertaker" and "The Stationmaster" are most revealing, since these two tales were written before or simultaneously with the foreword.

According to the neighbor's letter, Belkin was born in 1798, entered the service in 1815, retired and returned to his hereditary estate about 1823 (or more precisely in 1822). The tales were his first attempt at writing. On the basis of biographical data and certain of the neighbor's remarks, one can conclude that Ivan Petrovič finished writing his tales several years before he died, probably during the first years of his retirement in the country. In all probability he completed them by 1825 and devoted the next three years to his novel and other works.

The significance that Puškin attached to the precise correlation of all the tales with Belkin's biography can be ascertained from an examination of his manuscripts in which certain dates have been altered. These corrections are completely irrelevant to the tales themselves and can be explained only as Puskin's attempt to correlate the events in the tales with

93

the period of their writing by Belkin. What emerges are two completely different time systems: real time—1830—the "Boldino autumn" when Puškin himself worked on the tales and fictional time—1823-1825—when Belkin allegedly wrote his tales.

As mentioned above, it is certain only that "The Undertaker" was written earlier than the editor's foreword. The date alone on the manuscript of "The Stationmaster" is insufficient to determine whether Puškin wrote this tale before, after, or simultaneously with the foreword; both were finished on the same day—September 14. The remaining three tales were written after the forword; therefore, the problem of whether the internal chronology of the individual tales correlates with Belkin's biography arises only with respect to "The Undertaker" and "The Stationmaster."

In the manuscript of "The Undertaker," Puškin corrected a date in the fourth sentence:

> When he [Adrijan] crossed the unfamiliar threshold and found his new house in turmoil, he sighed for his old tumbledown hovel, where for the past eighteen years the strictest order had prevailed; . . .[2]

In the manuscript the number eighteen originally read "forty,"[3] and in the final version of the story, one may find an indirect explanation for this change in Puškin's reference to the fire of 1812 during the Napoleonic invasion: "The fire of 1812, which destroyed the ancient capital, also destroyed his [Jurko's] sentry box."[4] The burned police sentry box leads one to believe that Moscow was reduced to ashes down to the last pigeon coop. Obviously Puškin was referring to the Moscow fire in rather general terms, failing to consider that one-fourth of the buildings were, in fact, spared. Apparently, Adrijan Proxorov's wooden hovel burned down in the same fire, and thus the undertaker could not possibly have lived in his house for forty years by the beginning of the "Boldino autumn" in 1830. Therefore, Puškin changed "forty to eighteen (1812 + 18 = 1830). Undoubtedly at this point in the creative process Puškin still had no intention of introducing Belkin as the supposed author of the tales, for Belkin died in 1828.

The time scheme of "The Undertaker" attests to the fact that Puškin had no plans at that point for introducing an imaginary author at all. The inclusion of a fictitious author within a story requires either the use of *skaz* or the expansion of the time frame. In the latter case, according to convention, either the manuscript must be found, read, and delivered to the publisher, or the fictitious author must have the opportunity to pass

on his anecdote to the writer. The writer in turn must have a chance to
copy down the story. Puškin in his first draft allotted no time in "The
Undertaker" for these manipulations. Adrijan Proxorov lived for eighteen
years in his hovel and moved in 1830, the same year that Puškin wrote
the tale. This leaves no time for the introduction of a fictitious author.

In sharp contrast to the two-day adventure recounted in "The Undertaker," the chronology of "The Stationmaster" is more complex and
of many years' duration. The tale is related in the first person and hinges
on the narrator's three trips to the post-station of Samson Vyrin. The
action begins with A.G.N's first visit and ends with the third. The correlation between the internal chronology of the tale and Belkin's biography is contingent upon the time span of the story.

Approximately four years pass between the narrator's first and second visits to the post-station. When he meets the stationmaster the second
time, he is struck by the change he sees:

> It was certainly Samson Vyrin, but how he had aged! . . . I looked
> at his grey hair . . . and I was astonished that three or four years
> could have changed so healthy and cheerful a person into a feeble
> old man.[5]

Later the stationmaster's account of Dunja's flight begins with the words:
"Three years ago, one winter evening. . . ."[6] Narrator A.G.N. had arrived
at the station for the first time in May, and Minskij carried Dunja off in
the winter, apparently a year and a half from the day when A.G.N. kissed
the fourteen-year-old beauty in parting. At the end of the tale the young
boy who conducts A.G.N. to the stationmaster's grave recalls how Dunja
arrived "with three little boys and a wet nurse."[7] Thus one may ask
when her first child was born.

After Dunja's flight the stationmaster contracted a violent fever; "he
was taken to S***, and another stationmaster was appointed temporarily
in his place."[8] The fever could have lasted several months, as the drastic
change in Samson Vyrin's appearance which struck A.G.N. on his second
visit may suggest. Not until spring did the stationmaster recover from his
illness which was presumably brought on by nervous shock. Vyrin was
in Petersburg during the warmer months of the year when sleds were not
in use ("Suddenly an elegant carriage flashed by in front of him, and
the stationmaster recognized Minskij").[9] Somewhat later Vyrin enters
Dunja's apartment.

From his conversation with Minskij it becomes apparent that Dunja
was not married yet. If one assumes that Minskij married Dunja soon
after this scene and that she bore him three children within approximately

six years, it follows that at least seven years must have elapsed from the day she left her father's house until her arrival at his grave.

A.G.N. returned to the station for the last time a few months after Dunja. She arrived in the summer; he, in late autumn. To establish the period of time that elapsed between the first and final visits of A.G.N., that is, the duration of the entire tale, one need only add the year and a half that passed from the beginning of the tale until Dunja's elopement, the minimum of seven years of her life in Petersburg, and the few months between Dunja's and A.G.N.'s visits to the grave of the stationmaster. The time span amounts to approximately nine years. Concerning his last visit to the post-station, A.G.N. remarks: "Recently, while passing the town of ***, I remembered my friend."[10] Thus A.G.N. begins his narration soon after the actual tale has come to an end.

Twice Puškin altered the dates on which the events in the tale began, always shifting them further into the past. The years 1820 and 1819, which appeared in the manuscript,[11] were changed to 1816:

> In the month of May, 1816, I happened to be travelling through the province of *** on a road now no longer in existence.[12]

The original date appearing in the manuscript (1820), would have indicated that events culminated near the time of the "Boldino autumn" (1820 + 9 = 1829), thus reflecting the chronology of "The Undertaker."[13] The final date of 1816 correlates with Belkin's biography (1816 + 9 = 1825). In all likelihood Puškin made this revision on September 14, the day on which the foreword, "From the Editor," was completed. In the process of making this final correction, Puškin presumably also changed the date on which the tale itself was completed from September 13 to 14.[14]

"The Stationmaster" is the key tale in determining the process of organizing the entire cycle. It is the only tale in Puškin's manuscript in which the time of the ending was changed to conform with fictional (Belkin's) rather than real (Puškin's) time. Perhaps in coordinating the cycle of tales, Puškin deemed it necessary to assign their date of completion to a specific year in Belkin's life. He chose the year 1825 and, accordingly, changed the year in which "The Stationmaster" opens to 1816. However, in doing so, he neglected, as has been shown, to correlate the events of "The Undertaker" with Belkin's fictional biography and left the time frame of the story reflecting his own (Puškin's) date of writing the tale in the autumn of 1830.

The internal chronology of the remaining tales presents no such problem, as their dates fully accord with Belkin's biography. The action of "The Shot" spans the period from 1814 to 1820; "The Snowstorm," from 1811-1816; and "Mistress into Maid" takes place roughly in 1818.

The tales in the cycle can be divided into two groups: those presumably written before the image of Belkin had crystallized in Puškin's mind ("The Stationmaster" and "The Undertaker") and those written by Puškin with Belkin in mind ("The Shot," "The Snowstorm," and "Mistress into Maid"). This subdivision is based less upon when the tales were written than on when Puškin introduced a fictitious author. A clearly perceptible boundary separates the tales of the first and second groups. The first two tales focus on the lower class while the last three are concerned with the Russian nobility. In other words, as soon as the image of a fictitious author crystallized in Puškin's artistic plan, he introduced a broader social picture into the cycle.

Footnotes

1. Traditionally the foreword, "From the Editor," was thought to have been written much later in Moscow, from where Puškin wrote about his tales to P.A. Pletnev. It is dated, however, in the later edition of Puškin's works as September 14, 1830. See: P., v. 8, II, p. 1052.
2. P., v. 8, I, p. 89 (12).
3. Ibid., II, p. 625 (14-15).
4. Ibid., I, p. 91 (12).
5. Ibid., p. 100 (5).
6. Ibid.,(38).
7. Ibid., p. 106 (9).
8. Ibid., p. 102 (28).
9. Ibid., p. 104 (2).
10. Ibid., p. 105 (17).
11. Ibid., II, p. 642 (28-29) and p. 641 (15-16).
12. Ibid., I, p. 98 (15).
13. The time scheme of "The Undertaker," which lacks a fictional narrator, conforms more closely with Puškin's work in the "Boldino autumn" of 1830 than "The Stationmaster" whose narrator had to meet the writer (Puškin) and pass on to him his anecdote.
14. P., V. 8, II, p. 660 (below the manuscript).

Chapter 2

THE NARRATOR A.G.N.

There is a substantial difference between the narrative of "The Undertaker" and that of "The Stationmaster," the first two tales written by Puškin. "The Undertaker" is written in the third person, without a frame, and, separated from the cycle, might well sound like a story narrated by Puškin himself. "The Stationmaster," however, is told in the first person and is framed by the participation of Titular Counsellor A.G.N. This distinction is particularly important in view of the fact that either simultaneously with or immediately after Puškin completed "The Stationmaster," he wrote the foreword, "From the Editor," in which he introduced the same device of the fictitious author by which the entire cycle of tales is united. The figure of Titular Counsellor A.G.N. because of his several traits could well be termed as important as Vyrin and Dunja in "The Stationmaster." At this point, however, this analysis will concern itself with only one aspect of the man—namely, A.G.N. as a writer.

In "The Stationmaster," Puškin informs the reader for the first time that an entire cycle of tales is forthcoming. A.G.N. is the assumed author, and they are to be gathered from his traveling experiences throughout Russia. A.G.N. states: "Before long I hope to publish a curious collection of observations made during my travels."[1] Since Puškin wrote this passage before introducing Belkin as the author of the tales, it sounds very much as if A.G.N. were to become the narrator behind whom Puškin will conceal himself. What happened though was something very different: As if in haste, Puškin suddenly abandoned this particularly appealing narrator and, without revising the two already completed tales, created a different type of fictitious author. Not only does this result in a discrepancy between the internal chronology of "The Undertaker" and Belkin's biography, but a question as to Belkin's professional ethics arises.

Ivan Petrovič Belkin is presented in the foreword as a respectable and honest man who would not plagiarize. However, this is apparently exactly what happens through an oversight on Puškin's part. Belkin includes "The Stationmaster" in his cycle of stories despite the fact that the tale had been told to him by a fellow writer who had made it clear that he eventually intended to publish it himself. This inconsistency in

Belkin's character thus arose from Puškin's sudden change in his choice of fictitious authors. Apparently Puškin had initially designated the wandering Titular Counsellor A.G.N. as the "author" of his tales and at the last moment abandoned him in favor of Belkin. It seems that Puškin, while constructing his complex narrative scheme of six tales, overlooked two details which contradict Belkin's biography: first, the chronology in "The Undertaker" and second, A.G.N.'s intention to publish his travelogue.

There is additional evidence in "The Stationmaster" that indicates that Puškin, indeed, had initially chosen A.G.N. as the "author" of his tales. The original date for the beginning of the tale (1820) brought the outcome of events (1829) almost up to the "Boldino autumn" (1830). In order to set the tale within a frame, Puškin had to reserve some time for his meeting with A.G.N. He solved this problem neatly by ending the story close to the time of its actual recounting. A.G.N.'s concluding remarks, "Recently while passing through the town of ***, I remembered my friend,"[2] enable the events to retain their freshness in the mind of the narrator. Had A.G.N. remained the "author" of the entire cycle of stories, the proximity in time between his narration and their publication would have added to the sense of reality. Under the authorship of Belkin (who died in 1828), however, this device lost its force and became almost meaningless. The amount of time that elapsed between the events in the tales and their subsequent publication in 1831 ceased to be important.

Puškin's choice of Belkin was thus not his initial one. The genesis of the fictitious author was complex with Puškin's note, "On Popular Education," serving as one of its first stimuli. The idea took artistic shape in the character of A.G.N., whom Puškin then abandoned in search of a new figure who eventually became Belkin.

Footnotes

1. P., v. 8, I, pp. 97-98.
2. Ibid., p. 105 (17).

CHAPTER 3

BELKIN'S OTHER PREDECESSORS

In Puškin's entire oeuvre the name Belkin appears twice. Belkin is the author of the five short stories and the historian-author of Puškin's unfinished work, "The History of the Village of Gorjuxino." Among Puškin scholars the total separation of these two characters is at the present time a generally accepted fact. It suffices to add that these two Belkins have only three characteristics in common—they share a name, live in Gorjuxino, and both are fictional authors. The striking difference between them, however, can be illustrated by their literary product. Belkin, the historian, was meant by Puškin to write in all seriousness a grotesque history of a grotesque village while the Belkin of the editor's foreword produced five brilliant tales. This contrast in their literary product reflects also the difference in their cultural background and intellect and permits further examination of the genesis of Belkin, the author of the tales.

September 14 was obviously the decisive date in Puškin's work on the tales, since on this day another narrator, Titular Counsellor A.G.N., was considered for the role of fictitional author of the cycle. The pre-history of the narrator, A.G.N., is reflected in the fragment, "The Notes of a Young Man," dated approximately 1829-30, and presumably accessible to Puškin while he was writing "The Stationmaster."

A.G.N.'s reflections on the life and work of stationmasters are clearly linked to these "Notes," and Puškin almost literally copies from this fragment the narrator's description of the pictures on the walls of the stationmaster's house.[1] Thus the relationship between these two texts is certain, and since "The Notes of a Young Man" has no plot, its similarity to "The Stationmaster" must be defined in terms of the narrators—the young lieutenant of the "Notes" who only a few days earlier has graduated from a military school, and Titular Counsellor A.G.N.

There are, however, differences between these two narrators that in turn form an additional link between the two works. Titular Counsellor A.G.N. is significantly older and much more experienced than the young lieutenant who started writing travel sketches. The tone of their reactions to the world around them is totally different. A.G.N.'s attitude is

100

that of a sophisticated man whereas the young lieutenant acts like a recent graduate with curiosity and eagerness for adventure. This age difference, however, becomes a uniting rather than an alienating characteristic, since the Titular Counsellor's description of his experiences with
stationmasters in the past echoes those of the young lieutenant. Thus the
lieutenant is a portrait of A.G.N. years earlier when he was still young
and inexperienced while in A.G.N.'s personality one may detect the future portrait of the lieutenant. Several details support this hypothesis.
Both men belong to the educated class, and both have an inclination to
write. A.G.N. says so directly, and one knows that the young lieutenant
is writing his diary, or travel notes, and also that he intends to translate
from German into Russian the verses that he found on the pictures illus-
trating the parable of the prodigal son.

The relationship of these two narrators goes even further, however.
The political profile of A.G.N., his caustic comments on the current
social system in Russia and his rejection of the hierarchical structure of
the whole country based on the obsolete "Table of Ranks" have already
been established. The young lieutenant, of course, could not make such
political pronouncements, but some experiences which would probably
later lead him to a similar philosophy are outlined in the first lines of his
notes as they are found in Puškin's manuscript if all the corrections of the
author are taken into account:

> On May 4, 1825, I was promoted to the rank of officer of the
> Černigov regiment and on the 6th received the order to go to my
> regiment in the settlement Vasil'kovo in Kiev province—on the 9th
> I left Petersburg.[2]

Three important signs are concentrated in this concise account—1825, the
year of the Decembrists' revolt; the Černigov regiment, which revolted
on December 29, 1825, and was defeated on January 3, 1826; and the
town, Vasil'kov, which at that time served as revolutionary headquarters.
Puškin obviously intended to emphasize these revolutionary signs by introducing some implications on the same page:

> I still hear in my ears the noise and shouts of playing cadets and
> the monotonous humming of diligent pupils, who are repeating the
> vocabulary lesson—*le bluet, le bluet,* cornflower, *amarante,* amaranth,
> *amarante, amarante.* . . . Now the rattling of my carriage and ring-
> ing of the harness bells are the only sounds which break the sur-
> rounding silence.[3]

Thus amaranth, a flower the color of blood, and *le bluet,* or cornflower, which in Russian (*vasilek*) resembles the name of the town Vasil'kov, one of the centers of the southern branch of the revolutionary conspiracy, are introduced by Puškin in the very beginning of his unfinished story to foreshadow the adventures of the young lieutenant.

Puškin's intention to write a story about a young participant in revolutionary events is most important for the present study. Having established the direct relationship of this young officer to Titular Counsellor A.G.N., whom Puškin obviously considered the author of the five short stories, one sees that Belkin, who succeeded them as the author of the stories, is really an alloy of Puškin's two separate attempts to create a fictitious author.

To present a full picture of Puškin's search for the character who would realize his intention, one must turn finally to the first draft of A.P.'s foreword.[4] This fragment consists exclusively of an excerpt from the neighbor's letter about the author of the tales. The first two paragraphs of this letter contain important dates for the present study. The author of the manuscript is not I. P. Belkin yet but rather Petr Ivanovič D. He was born in 1801 (the same year as Belkin, the historian) and is thus older than the young lieutenant and younger than I. P. Belkin, who was born in 1798. Petr Ivanovič D. actually has very little in common with I. P. Belkin except for the fact that his estate is also in Gorjuxino and that he does not follow tradition in managing his serfs. He is much better educated than Belkin; he graduated from a military school and was appointed to the Selenginsk infantry regiment in which he served until 1822. The name, Selenginsk, acquires significance if one recalls that Major Gaevskij with whom Puškin was acquainted in Kišinov was serving in this regiment, where he was sent from the Semenov Imperial Guard regiment after the rebellion.[5]

Thus Petr Ivanovič D. had two important relationships: one with the lieutenant who wrote "Notes of a Young man," and the second with I. P. Belkin, the historian. The former relationship is based on their military education and service which eventually likely brought them into contact with the southern branch of the Decembrists; the second relationship is based on eccentric behavior, real or alleged mismanagement of an estate, and an extraordinary passion for literary work. Since the identity of the author of the tales has diverged from that of Petr Ivanovič D., Puškin presumably blended into one fictitious author two images—Belkin, a young man who by chance and by his station during military service, became involved in revolutionary events directly related to the Decembrist movement, and an eccentric, a representative of the landed gentry, a self-made writer and historian. I. P. Belkin, the story writer, obviously combines all these characteristics. Puškin adapted the naive and intellectually limited Belkin, the historian, to the image of the author of the five tales as a shield for the other side of his personality, which Petr Ivanovič D., Titular Counseller A.G.N., and the young lieutenant in "The Notes of a Young Man" embody.

Though Ivan Petrovič Belkin, the story writer, is only superficially linked with the comical Belkin, the historian, this hindered literary critics from correctly assessing the "author" of the tales and prevented the reader from perceiving in the neighbor's description those characteristics that link him with Titular Counsellor A.G.N., Petr Ivanovič D., and the young lieutenant. Puškin apparently never intended to present two Belkins in his works, and should he have decided to finish "The History of the Village of Gorjuxino," it is likely he would have changed the name of the author and the village.

Footnotes

1. In Puškin's manuscript of "The Stationmaster" there is a phrase, "from 'The Notes of a Young Man,'" and in the manuscript of "The Notes" a section with a description of the pictures on the wall of the post-station is marked by a line in the margin. See: P., v. 8, II, p. 642, and p. 949, footnote.
2. Ibid., I, p. 403 (2-4).
3. Ibid., p. 403 (10-15).
4. Ibid., II, pp. 581-583.
5. I. P. Liprandi, "Iz denvnika i vospominanij," *A. S. Puškin v vospominanijax sovremennikov*, M., 1974, p. 298. See also: Chapter I, section 1 in the present book.

Chapter 4

PUŠKIN'S ANONYMITY

It is commonly accepted that Puškin wished to remain anonymous in the first edition of the tales. Actually, this is inaccurate. Although Puškin published his tales anonymously, he did not mask his authorship entirely. Such a strategy, as will soon become clear, was not without good reason.

Returning from Boldino to Moscow, Puškin sent a curious account of his work in the country to his friend and publisher in Petersburg, N. A. Pletnev. This letter dated December 9, 1830, contains the first extant references to *The Tales of Belkin*:

> I shall tell you (as a secret) that in Boldino I wrote as I have not written for a long time. Here is what I have brought along: the *last* two chapters of Onegin, the eighth and ninth, completely ready for the press. A tale, written in ottava rima (of about 400 verses), which let's bring out anonymously. Several dramatic scenes or little tragedies, namely: *The Avaricious Knight, Mozart and Salieri, Feast in the Time of the Plague,* and *Don Juan.* In addition to that, I have written about 30 small poems. Good? That is still not all (completely secret).* I have written five prose tales which are making Baratynskij hee-haw and kick about—and which we shall also publish anonymously. It will be impossible under my name, for Bulgarin would rail. And so Russian literature has been delivered up, head, neck, and ears, to Bulgarin and Greč! . . .
> *For you alone.[1]

Clearly Puškin planned to publish both *The Tales of Belkin* and "The Little House in Kolomna" (the tale written in ottava rima) anonymously. He mentions the latter casually but pauses on *The Tales of Belkin*, emphasizing the confidential nature of this information ("completely secret," to which he adds the footnote "for you alone") and explains his decision to publish them anonymously ("Bulgarin would rail"). The remark, "five prose tales which are making Baratynskij hee-haw and kick about . . .," contains an intriguing innuendo: what was it in the tales that so amused Baratynskij? Furthermore, what was the connection between the two anonymous publications mentioned in the letter, and why did Puškin specifically comment on *The Tales of Belkin?*

"The Little House in Kolomna" was, in fact, never published anonymously. It appeared in 1833 under Puškin's name and was heavily abridged, since certain polemical passages had already lost their sting by then. There is no doubt, however, that Puškin originally intended to publish this work anonymously precisely because of the controversial nature of its subject. But what exactly necessitated the anonymous publication of *The Tales of Belkin?* Was it simply that "Bulgarin would rail," or were there risks in this work as well? If one assumes that Puškin did not, in fact, present the full picture to Pletnev or reveal his real reasons for wishing to publish the tales anonymously, what then was his motive for concealing his authorship?

From Puškin's correspondence with Pletnev between December 9, 1830, and August 15, 1831, the history of the publication of *The Tales of Belkin* can be outlined. The first mention of the tales occurs in Puškin's letter of December 9 expressing his desire and his reason (whether true or alleged remains to be seen) for anonymity.

In a letter of February 16, 1831, to Pletnev, Puškin, describing the financial difficulties caused by his approaching marriage, concludes: "There is nothing else to do: I shall have to print my tales. I'll send them to you next week, and let's print them by Easter."[2] One may sense a certain reluctance on Puškin's part to publish his five tales, which were listed with obvious pride in his letter of December 9, 1830. Puškin, however, did not keep his promise and obviously did not send his tales to Pletnev in a week. On July 3, 1831, the tales were still in Puškin's hands: "I have copied my five tales and the foreword, i.e., the compositions of the late Belkin, a fine fellow. What do you want me to do with them? Shall we print them ourselves, or shall we make a bargain with Smirdin? R.S.V.P."[3] This is the first reference to a foreword to the tales. Apparently Puškin considered it to be ready for publication, yet in his next letter to Pletnev, on July 11, 1831, Puškin notes that he is sending the tales separately from the foreword:

A few days ago I sent off to you via Esling the tales of my friend, the late Belkin. Have you received them? I shall furnish the foreword later. Submit them to the censor—the civil one, not that of the emperor—and let's sniff out an understanding with Smirdin. I am of the opinion that these tales can bring us in 10,000—and here is how:

    2,000 copies at 6 rubles = 12,000
    − 1,000 for printing
    − 1,000 commission

                                                      Net 10,000.[4]

Puškin's estimate, as usual too optimistic, reflects those financial difficulties which he outlined in his letter of February 16, 1831. As far as the tales themselves are concerned, Puškin's plan to send them to Pletnev without the foreword, may have a direct bearing on the following sentence in which he urges Pletnev to send the tales to the regular censor rather than to Count Benkendorf for the emperor's personal scrutiny. It seems that Puškin either had intended to send his work to the censor in two instalments—the five tales and later the foreword under separate cover—or that he intended to publish his tales without submitting the foreword to the censor at all. In both cases the censor would have received from Pletnev a manuscript written by the late, unknown author, I. P. Belkin. Neither intention was realized at this point, since, as Puškin's letter of August 3, 1831, indicates, the tales did not reach Pletnev: "My tales returned to me, without reaching you."[5] One also learns about Èsling's failure to deliver Puškin's tales to Pletnev from the latter's letter of July 19, 1931: "Esling (only God knows who is this creature! You must have got the idea that I am acquainted with the entire world) I have not seen, and I have not heard anything about the tales. I shall be glad to publish them but only after my return to the city, i.e. after the cholera is gone. . . ."[6]

Approximately by August 15, 1831, Puškin still had not sent his foreword to Pletnev: "I am sending you by Gogol the tales of my friend Ivan Petrovič Belkin: submit them to the regular censor, and let's proceed with their publication. I shall send the foreword later."[7] This passage is almost word for word a repetition of the excerpt from Puškin's letter of July 11, 1831. The most striking similarity between these two passages is the proximity of Puškin's promise to send the foreword later and his insistence that the five tales be sent to the regular censor obviously without the foreword. At this point Puškin's plan has succeeded, for Pletnev in his letter of September 5, 1831, writes: "The tales of Ivan Petrovič Belkin returned from the censor. . . . Won't you delay publication by [procrastinating in] sending the Foreword and the hilarious epigraph?"[8] Puškin did not delay the publication of Belkin's tales, since by the end of October, 1831, they were published by Smirdin with the permission of the censor, N. I. Butyrskij, who apparently never had the opportunity to read the foreword.

It appears quite clear that Puškin deliberately postponed sending his foreword to Pletnev, not because it was unfinished, but rather because he intended to evade the censor. Thus Puškin twice violated government regulations: first he broke his promise to submit all his new works for the emperor's personal censorship, and, secondly, to the regular censor he submitted only a part of his work. Puškin, however, remained anonymous only to the government. For his readers he chose a different tactic. In his letter of August 15, 1831 to Pletnev, Puškin wrote: "Whisper my name to Smirdin, for him to whisper it on to purchasers."[9] This arrangement, of course, was due to Puškin's financial hardship. He intended to promote his book under the name of the real author, which for some reason had to be concealed from the government.

Although only limited facts are available, they are sufficient to shed some light on the history of the publication of the tales. Puškin did not preserve strict anonymity even in the first edition of the tales, and subsequently they appeared in a prose collection under his name. This fact all but refutes Puškin's letter to Pletnev of December 9, 1830, regarding the reason for publishing the tales anonymously. Obviously "Bulgarin would rail" over the second edition of the tales as much as he would have ranted about the first.

Puškin's letter to Pletnev referred to the first edition of the tales which appeared in print in 1831. The title page of this edition reads as follows: "The Tales of the late Ivan Petrovič Belkin, published by A.P." Any reader of that time, and certainly one close to literary circles (and all the more so Bulgarin), surely would have been able to identify the author whose initials were A.P. Puškin had published some of his poems under his initials many times in journals and other literary miscellanies, and upon occasion the same verses appeared in the table of contents under his full name. After all these considerations one must conclude that Puškin was not candid in his letter of December 9, 1830, to Pletnev and used Bulgarin's presumed reaction merely as a pretext for anonymity. In fact, Puškin was desperately trying to avoid submission of the foreword to any censor and especially to the emperor.

Three years later, on or about April 9, 1834, having decided to reissue *The Tales of Belkin*, Puškin wrote to the censor, A. Nikitenko:

> May I rely on your benevolence? I want to publish *The Tales of Belkin* in a second edition, adding to it 'The Queen of Spades' and a few other previously published works. Could you let all of this pass? I shall be most grateful to you.[10]

By mentioning the fact that all the works had already been published, Puškin suggests prior censorship. Nikitenko, therefore, considering his scrutiny of the tales with the foreword a mere formality, likely only skimmed them. The foreword, however, which had been published in 1831 without ever having been submitted to the censor, thus escaped censorship for the second time in 1834.

It appears that Puškin had employed three tactics in his endeavor to publish *The Tales of Belkin*: He misinformed his close friend, P. A. Pletnev, why he wished to remain anonymous, directed the five tales to the ordinary censor carefully avoiding Nicholas I and, more specifically, the office of Count Benkendorf, and furthermore he did everything in his power to smuggle the foreword of the fictional editor, A.P., past the censors. Thus one may conclude that the foreword dealing with I. P. Belkin was most important to Puškin and the real reason for his anonymity.

Footnotes

1. P., v. 14, p. 133. (See also English translation in *The Letters of Alexander Pushkin*, translated by J. Thomas Shaw, University of Wisconsin Press, 1967, p. 446.
2. Ibid., p. 152. (J. T. Shaw, p. 459.)
3. Ibid., p. 186. (J. T. Shaw, p. 498.)
4. Ibid., p. 189. (J. T. Shaw, p. 501.)
5. Ibid., p. 206. (J. T. Shaw, p. 522.)
6. Ibid., p. 195.
7. Ibid., p. 209. (J. T. Shaw, p. 524.)
8. Ibid., p. 221.
9. Ibid., p. 209. (J. T. Shaw, p. 524.)
10. Ibid., v. 15, p. 124.

POSTSCRIPT

THE CURIOUS RESARCHERS

There is some evidence to support the hypothesis that *The Tales of Belkin* was at least partially deciphered by Puškin's own contemporaries. One of the "curious researchers" was the editor of *The Northern Bee*, Faddej Bulgarin. In his review of *The Tales* in the issue of November 10, 1831, he wrote:

> In this book there are six anecdotes, adventures, horrifying events whatever you want to call them—narrated masterfully: rapidly, vividly, ardently, captivatingly.[1]

That Bulgarin correctly understood the tales is suggested in his mentioning six "anecdotes." Bulgarin obviously discerned an independent plot in the foreword that transformed it into a tale in his eyes. His keen insight is apparent in another section of the review:

> The narrator does not tire you out with details that would be appropriate only in a real tale; he sketches his images lightly, but he flings these details at us discriminatingly; each one is vital for the composition of the whole; sometimes he forgets his role as narrator, and for several minutes he himself becomes a character, supplanting his narrative pictures with a dramatic scene, and, thus, his facial expression, his voice, and the style of his speech change.[2]

The most significant and interesting observations in the review are somewhat enigmatic. Had Bulgarin not noticed A.G.N.'s sarcastic intonation in his remarks on rank and intelligence, he could not have discerned that the narrator had become a character and had extended his narration into a dramatic scene, thereby changing his "facial expression" and voice. Bulgarin's comments assume importance if he did, indeed, treat the tales as an artistic whole. The apparent absurdities in the review are proof of the fact that Bulgarin penetrated the smoke screen of the complex code and showed himself to be one of the most discerning readers of his time. He was justified in implying that both the narrator's expression and voice fluctuate in the introduction to "The Stationmaster." He was also right in maintaining that the author introduced the details very selectively for the benefit of the "composition of the whole." For Bulgarin, of course, this "whole" comprised "six anecdotes," including the foreword. There can be no doubt that Bulgarin composed his elliptical lines specifically for Puškin, as the average reader of the time would not have understood Bulgarin's implications.

Bulgarin was not only suspicious of Belkin's authorship of the tales but continually questioned the justification for this device, or "maneuver," as he called it. Specifically he had in mind A.G.N.'s judgment on rank and intelligence. He regretted that the prologue to "The Stationmaster" had not been written in verse and felt that the description of the station and stationmasters

> perhaps would be pleasing . . . if it were *supported by a flying rhyme* [sic], but in prose it is limp, inexpressive, and—to tell the truth—boring.[3]

Bulgarin apparently had two intentions. He wanted to suggest that Puškin, who wrote "concisely, vividly, ardently and captivatingly," introduced this somewhat sluggish passage into the tale for extra-literary reasons, but primarily he wanted to slip in a quote from Puškin's poem, "The Prose Writer and the Poet." It is not inconceivable that Bulgarin may have intended to threaten Puškin by including a quote from this poem in his review. Puškin, of course, well understood the implications of the excerpt quoted by Bulgarin. The poem reads:

> What are you troubled about, prose writer?
> Give me an idea, whatever you like:
> I will sharpen its point,
> I will feather it with a flying rhyme,
> I will lay it on a taut bowstring,
> I will bend my obedient bow into an arc,
> And then I will send it boldly,
> And woe to our enemy![4]

Bulgarin's allusion is clear; he understood Puškin's mockery perfectly, and the analogy between the passage from "The Stationmaster" and a sharpened arrow shot straight at an enemy is apt.

In a completely different setting, in the prison at the Petrovskij Zavod in Siberia, the Decembrists also read *The Tales of Belkin* and understood them fully. The Decembrists were forbidden to correspond with anyone in Russia. Despite the obstacles, the distance, and the police barriers, however, sufficient evidence emerged from remote Siberia to indicate that the prisoners there indeed had understood *The Tales of Belkin*. Princess

Marja Nikolaevna Volkonskaja, wife of the Decembrist, S. G. Volkonskij, wrote the following to S. N. Raevskaja on February 19, 1832, from Petrovskij Zavod:

> The tales of Puškin, the so-called Belkin, are a real event here. There is nothing more enticing and harmonious than this prose. Everything in it is a tableau. He has opened new paths to our writers.[5]

The Tales of Belkin were published toward the end of October, 1831. Just four months later Princess Volkonskaja was writing about them from Siberia, and from her brief note it is clear that the tales had already been read and discussed by the Decembrists in the prison at the Petrovskij Zavod in which there were sixty-five men. If the slow mails between the principal cities and Siberia are taken into account, one can imagine how quickly and avidly Puškin's new book was read and debated.

The Decembrists in Siberia did not suffer from a paucity of books or periodicals. All the literary news reached them, and their taste did not lag behind that of their contemporaries living in both capitals of Russia. The imprisoned Decembrists, however, differing with the published critics of the time (including Belinskij) who considered *The Tales of Belkin* proof of the decline of Puškin's genius, praised it highly; for the Decembrists it was, indeed, an event.

Belkin's liberation of the Gorjuxino peasants could not have gone unnoticed by the Decembrists, some of whom had already converted their serfs from the system of corvée to one of modest quit-rents, thus freeing them economically even before the uprising of 1825. Neither could the reference to the Lancaster system of instruction in "Mistress into Maid" go unheeded nor the quotation from Griboedov's comedy, *Woe from Wit*, in "The Snowstorm."

A deciphering of the tales could not possibly have appeared in Princess Volkonskaja's letter. That the Decembrists themselves were prevented from corresponding meant that the letters of their wives in which the thoughts of the prisoners found reflection were closely watched. The letters had to be submitted to the officer on duty after which they were passed on to the warden for examination, were then sent to the governor of the province, and finally arrived at the Third Department of the Chancellery of His Majesty, i.e., Count Benkendorf's. From Princess Volkonskaja's letter Benkendorf could have learned that *The Tales of Belkin* was a new work by Puškin, who had published it without first presenting it for examination to his personal censor, Nicholas I. Whether Count Benkendorf was aware that Puškin had broken his promise to send all of his new works to the emperor for examination is not known. In any event Princess Volkonskaja's mention of Puškin's name was careless. In evaluating *The Tales of Belkin*, however, she was much more cautious, limiting herself to describing the impression made on the Decembrists by the tales and calling them only a "real event." In order to become an "event" for well-educated, demanding readers, and the Decembrists undoubtedly were, *The Tales of Belkin* had to be something more than amusing anecdotes. In order to appreciate these tales, such readers had to find more profundity in them, and they could do this only by decoding the cycle.

As subtle and discerning a judge of art as Princess Volkonskaja would not likely have made the commonplace observation that Puškin's tales were a "tableau." What was important to convey and what Princess Volkonskaja no doubt was describing was the fact that every detail in Puškin's work was a faithful depiction of historical reality. In the phrase, "Everything in it is a tableau," obviously she was referring to the foreword, "From the Editor."

Princess Volkonskaja also wrote that Puškin "opened new paths to our writers." What the princess meant by "new paths" may well be that method of veiling certain references forbidden by the censor; that is, the coded message to the "curious researchers." It is not surprising that Puškin's success in dealing with these topics constituted an "event" for the imprisoned Decembrists. They presumably not only deciphered *The Tales* but also analyzed the code which they took to be a new phenomenon in literature necessitated by rigorous censorship. The Decembrists might have been hopeful than Puškin's subtle method of portraying historical reality would find followers.

Footnotes

1. P. N. Stolpjanskij, "Puškin i Severnaja Pčela," *Puškin i ego sovremenniki*, Petrograd, 1916, XXIII-XXIV, p. 178.
2. Ibid., p. 177.
3. Ibid., 1927, XXXI-XXXII, p. 134.
4. Published in 1827, P., v. 2, I, p. 444.
5. M. P. Sultan-Šax, "M. N. Volkonskaja o Puškine v ee pis'max, 1830-1832 godov," *Puškin, issledovanija i materialy*, M.-L., 1956, v. 1, p. 266.